OPERATIONAL CERTIFICATION PROCEDURES OF FREE TRADE AGREEMENTS IN ASIA

AN IN-DEPTH ANALYSIS FOR IMPLEMENTING TRADE FACILITATION REFORMS

Pramila Crivelli, Stefano Inama, and Mark Pearson

DECEMBER 2024

ASIAN DEVELOPMENT BANK

ADB

6 ADB Avenue, Mandaluyong City, 1550 Metro Manila, Philippines
Tel +63 2 8632 4444; Fax +63 2 8636 2444
www.adb.org

ISBN 978-92-9277-065-5 (print); 978-92-9277-066-2 (PDF); 978-92-9277-067-9 (ebook)
Publication Stock No. TCS240574-2
DOI: http://dx.doi.org/10.22617/TCS240574-2

Notes:
In this publication, "€" refers to the euro, "¥" to the Japanese yen, and "$" refers to United States dollar.
ADB recognizes "China" as the People's Republic of China, "Korea" as the Republic of Korea, and "Vietnam" as Viet Nam.

Cover design by Michael Cortes.

Contents

Tables, Figures, and Boxes

Tables

Figures

Boxes

Acknowledgments

This report was prepared by the Regional Cooperation and Integration Division (ERCI) of the Economic Research and Development Impact Department (ERDI) of the Asian Development Bank (ADB). It was supported by the ADB technical assistance project, TA 6740: Raising the Value of Regional Trade Agreements—Key Factors for Successful Implementation and Positive Economic Impact, financed by ADB's Technical Assistance Special Fund and the Regional Cooperation and Integration Fund.

The report was authored by Pramila Crivelli, economist in ERCI; Stefano Inama, chief at the United Nations Conference on Trade and Development; and Mark Pearson, ADB consultant. Authors are grateful for the specific contributions and expert peer review provided by representatives from the private sector and customs officials in Asia and the Pacific, including Massimo Trabucco (Nestlé), Kit Hickey (Fonterra), Michel Anliker (Schindler), former New Zealand customs official Saba Vallipuram, Roberto Soprano (Aramco), Lilia Lopez (Ingredion), and Pier Paolo Ghetti (Deloitte).

Paulo Rodelio Halili and Pramila Crivelli coordinated the production of this report under the supervision of Jong Woo Kang, director, ERCI.

James Unwin edited the manuscript, and Michael Cortes created the cover design and implemented the typesetting and layout. Lawrence Casiraya proofread the report. Amiel Bryan Esperanza assisted in the coordination of peer review sessions. The Printing Services Unit of ADB's Corporate Services Department and the Publishing Team of the Department of Communications and Knowledge Management provided printing and publishing support.

Abbreviations

AANZFTA	ASEAN–Australia–New Zealand Free Trade Area
ACFTA	ASEAN–China Free Trade Area
ADB	Asian Development Bank
AFTA	ASEAN Free Trade Area
AJCEP	ASEAN–Japan Comprehensive Economic Partnership
AKFTA	ASEAN–Korea Free Trade Area
ARO	Agreement on Rules of Origin
ASEAN	Association of Southeast Asian Nations
ATIGA	ASEAN Trade in Goods Agreement
B/L	bill of lading
CEP	Closer Economic Partnership
CETA	Comprehensive Economic and Trade Agreement
CO	certificate of origin
CPTPP	Comprehensive and Progressive Agreement for Trans-Pacific Partnership
CTC	Change in Tariff Classification
e-CO	electronic certificate of origin
EODES	Electronic Origin Data Exchange System
EU	European Union
FOB	free on board
FTA	free trade agreement
GSP	Generalized System of Preferences
Lao PDR	Lao People's Democratic Republic
LDC	least developed country
OCP	operational certification procedures
PSRO	product-specific rules of origin
RCEP	Regional Comprehensive Economic Partnership
REX	Registered Exporter
RKC	Revised Kyoto Convention
RVC	regional value content
SCAROO	Subcommittee on ATIGA Rules of Origin
SCPP	Self-Certification Pilot Project
UNCTAD	United Nations Conference on Trade and Development
WCO	World Customs Organization
WTO	World Trade Organization

1. Introduction

This study is part of a systemic research program focusing on rules of origin in Asia and the Pacific, which stems from the expectations raised by the entry into force of the Regional Comprehensive Economic Partnership (RCEP). RCEP's common rules of origin platform was expected to unravel the "noodle bowl" effect of overlapping free trade agreements (FTAs).

In an initial Asian Development Bank (ADB) study of RCEP product-specific rules of origin (PSRO), Crivelli, Inama, and Pearson (2022) found RCEP PSRO not to be the most liberal compared with the PSRO of the Association of Southeast Asian Nations (ASEAN) Trade in Goods Agreement (ATIGA) and of the mega-regional Comprehensive and Progressive Agreement for Trans-Pacific Partnership (CPTPP).

This analysis was complemented by comparing the PSROs of RCEP with those of the ASEAN Plus One free trade agreements (ASEAN+1 FTAs),[1] since RCEP can be considered the natural evolution of initiatives between ASEAN and its dialogue partners. Once again, RCEP PSRO were found not to be the most liberal. The ASEAN–Australia–New Zealand Free Trade Agreement (AANZFTA), for instance, contained more liberal PSRO than RCEP (Crivelli, Inama, and Pearson 2023).

Importantly, both studies found significant scope for convergence since many of the examined FTAs contained similar PSRO requirements. PSROs were examined according to their substantive requirements, rather than on the form in which they are expressed. Accordingly, wide scope exists for progressively advocating the alignment and convergence of PSROs in different FTAs for sectors where convergence has been identified.

However, complexity over rules of origin and the intricacy of the noodle bowl are not limited to PSROs. This study covers another element of rules of origin, known in jargon of the Asia and Pacific region as operational certification procedures (OCPs). These are commonly referred to as "proof of origin" in many other administrations and FTAs.

Each FTA in Asia and the Pacific not only has a different set of PSROs but also different OCPs. Compliance generates costs for firms. As an illustration of such complexity, the website of the RCEP Secretariat lists[2] two methods of CO issuance – paper-based original copy or digital format CO[3] – and four different ways of presenting a certificate of origin (CO) to customs authorities in member states (1) a paper-based

1 ASEAN+1 FTAs are agreements establishing free trade areas between ASEAN member economies as a group and individual non-ASEAN dialogue partners, including Australia; the People's Republic of China (PRC); Hong Kong, China; India; Japan; and New Zealand; and the Republic of Korea.

2 See RCEP Parties' and Signatory States' Status on CO Issuance and CO/DO Acceptance at the EIF (as of 15 July 2024) at https://rcepsec.org/wp-content/uploads/2024/08/6-RCEP-Parties-and-Signatory-States-Status-on-electronic-CO-issuance-and-PO-acceptance_15-August-2024-rev.pdf.

3 Digital format CO means that the CO is issued in image file such as PDF and JPEG which complies with RCEP CO form including signature and official seal of the issuing body.

original copy, (2) a paper-based scanned copy, which is a printed hard copy of the scanned file, such as PDF and JPEG, from the paper-based original copy (3) a self-printed copy , which is a digital format CO printed in a paper by traders, and (4) a certificate of origin in electronic format (e-CO), which means that the CO/DO is accepted in electronic format at the customs. This may cover eCO and scanned file (such as PDF and JPEG) of paper-based original copy (e-CO). According to the website, each of the 15 RCEP member states is found to have different practices for accepting or issuing the four types. In addition, various versions of the document describing the CO Issuance and CO/DO Acceptance have appeared on the website since the RCEP's entry into force. Most importantly, these variations in the presentation of COs do not align with the legal text of the RCEP.

OCPs may also be described as administrative procedures and documentary evidence to be presented at customs to prove the origin of goods. A CO is the most glaring and common example. In reality, OCPs cover many other provisions such as those proving how goods have been shipped and related to the required accompanying documents for customs clearance.

Countries in Asia and the Pacific have been active in developing different OCPs. First, a number of different CO forms have been developed together with ancillary requirements—which means that each ASEAN+1 FTA has a different one. Lately, with the consequences of this complexity becoming progressively more apparent, initiatives have been undertaken to simplify OPCs by introducing IT and digital solutions like electronic certificates of origin (e-COs).

Such solutions are as diverse as the number of different COs previously developed and are overlapping. Different schools of thought are developing over the best solution or practice for addressing proof of origin and OCP issues. These are discussed in this study with a view to identifying policy recommendations.

This study complements the findings of previous ADB publications by comparing not only OCPs contained in the RCEP, the CPTPP, and ASEAN+1 FTAs, but also other best practices contained in FTAs that Asian countries have entered into with the European Union (EU) and the United States (US). This assessment compares the different OCP provisions in these agreements by assigning them a code related to the leniency and/or stringency of their compliance requirements. Whenever possible, the scope for convergence among OCPs used in FTAs is identified.

Together with previous studies on PSROs, this study offers actionable policy options for ASEAN to make tangible progress toward trade-facilitating rules of origin and OCPs. It has been peer reviewed by private sector representatives and former customs officials in Asia and the Pacific.[4]

4 Massimo Trabucco of Nestlé, Kit Hickey of Fonterra, Michel Anliker of Schindler, the former New Zealand customs official Saba Vallipuram, Roberto Soprano of Aramco, Lilia Lopez of Ingredion, and Pier Paolo Ghetti of Deloitte.

2. Multilateral Rules on Proof of Origin: Annex K of the Revised Kyoto Convention and Generalized System of Preferences Form A

The only multilateral instrument providing definitions and containing related procedures related to proof of origin is Annex K of the Revised Kyoto Convention (RKC).[5] The World Trade Organization (WTO) Agreement on Rules of Origin (ARO) is in fact silent on administrative issues related to rules of origin, nor in recent years has any attempt been carried out to initiate discussions.

Annex K of the Revised Kyoto Convention of the World Customs Organization (WCO) contains three chapters: Chapter 1, Rules of Origin; Chapter 2, Documentary Evidence of Origin; and Chapter 3, Control of Documentary Evidence of Origin. The annex also contains a specimen form of a certificate of origin.

The major limitation of Annex K is that it dates from the 1970s and a revision made in 1999. The revision of 1999 offers a limited scope since the expectation was that the entry into force of the Harmonization Work Program (HWP) of non-preferential rules of origin under the ARO would have provided the opportunity to establish a multilateral framework. However, lack of consensus on finalizing the HWP resulted in a stalemate with implications on any attempt to set a multilateral framework on rules of origin. As a result, Annex K of the RKC is outdated and the ARO does not provide a multilateral framework on rules of origin (see Crivelli and Inama 2022).

In May 2018, the RKC Management Committee approved a plan to update RKC and its annexes, recognizing the need to ensure that RKC maintains its relevance. Within this framework, a sponsoring group of countries has developed a proposal to update Annex K on rules of origin.[6]

According to its proponents, the new Specific Annex K would provide a "toolbox," building on the WCO Origin Compendium 2017 and other relevant literature and research. This plurilateral instrument will establish clear concepts and definitions of origin rules and procedures using a "common language" and a common meaning. The instrument will be making it easier for customs, other competent authorities, and stakeholders to understand and apply the rules and procedures.

Although the proponents have made progress in developing the revised text of Annex K, the overall pace of updating the RKC has been slow and the proponents are exploring possible avenues to finalize the new text of Annex K and its eventual adoption as a plurilateral agreement.

---

5 World Customs Organization, Specific Annex K, 17 April 2008. https://www.wcoomd.org/en/topics/facilitation/instrument-and-tools/conventions/pf_revised_kyoto_conv/kyoto_new/spank.aspx.

6 The sponsoring group is composed of Australia, the EU, the Eurasian Economic Community, the PRC, Japan, New Zealand, Norway, Switzerland, the United Nations Conference on Trade and Development (UNCTAD), and private sector companies (Nissan, Renault, and Fonterra).

Besides the attempt of updating Annex K, the WCO has elaborated other multilateral reference materials such as the Guidelines on Certification (WCO 2018). Recent studies, namely, a study on the digitalization of the certificates of origin and a feasibility study for an interconnectivity framework for certificates of origin, were presented for discussion in February 2023 at the WCO's Technical Committee on Rules of Origin (WCO 2024a, 2024b)

Besides WCO efforts to establish a multilateral framework for rules of origin, the United Nations Conference on Trade and Development (UNCTAD) intergovernmental machinery under the Generalized System of Preferences (GSP) initiative managed in 1968 to produce the first multilaterally agreed preferential certificate of origin: the GSP Form A.[7]

GSP Form A has been used for decades by the majority of preference-giving countries as the main documentary evidence to prove origin under the GSP, and is still used at present. As such, Form A may be considered to be a valid benchmark to measure the complexity of other existing certificate of origin forms elaborated in different FTAs.[8] While GSP Form A is a proof of origin in the context of unilateral trade preferences and not FTAs, it was the first multilaterally agreed form and has been in use since the 1970s, before the drive for FTAs began. Thus, Form A represents a legitimate comparison test for other forms used in the context of FTAs since it has the same purpose: documentary proof of origin.

The most recent other multilateral instruments setting best practices for encouraging self-certification of proof of origin are the WTO Bali and Nairobi ministerial Decisions on preferential rules of origin for Least Developed Countries (LDCs).

Part B of the WTO Bali Decision on preferential rules of origin for LDCs is dedicated to documentary requirements that clearly outline desired best practices that could be adopted by preference-granting countries when implementing rules of origin for LDCs.

Paragraph 1.8 reiterates the preference for self-certification:

"The documentary requirements regarding compliance with the rules of origin should be simple and transparent. For instance, the requirement to provide proof of non-manipulation or any other prescribed form for a certification of origin for products shipped from LDCs across other Members may be avoided. With regard to certification of rules of origin, whenever possible, self-certification may be recognized. Mutual customs cooperation and monitoring could complement compliance and risk-management measures."

The subsequent Nairobi Decision also reiterates the call to allow self-certification and the need for simplification for the documentary evidence related to direct consignment of goods for LDCs to the preference-granting countries:

7 See Annex 1 for a specimen of the GSP Form A.

8 Although GSP could be used as a benchmark, it should be noted that there is a huge difference between GSP andFTAs. GSP is a nonreciprocal arrangement, whereas FTAs are agreements among or between parties. Differences in OCPs are negotiated outcomes.

"3. Documentary requirements

3.1. With a view to reducing the administrative burden related to documentary and procedural requirements related to origin, Preference-granting Members shall:

- *a) As a general principle, refrain from requiring a certificate of non-manipulation for products originating in a LDC but shipped across other countries unless there are concerns regarding transshipment, manipulation, or fraudulent documentation; and*
- *b) Consider other measures to further streamline customs procedures, such as minimizing documentation requirements for small consignments or allowing for self-certification."*

Subsequent submissions by the LDC WTO group on the preferred modalities to implement the Bali and Nairobi ministerial Decisions pointed out that major preference-granting countries are moving toward allowing self-certification[9] and moving forward on best practices to be adopted for documentary evidence of direct consignment.[10]

9 See the LDC WTO group submissions to the WTO Committee on Rules of Origin: Examination of Existing Origin-Related Documentary Requirements, WTO document G/RO/W/211, 25 March 2022; and Direct Consignment Rules and Low Utilization of Trade Preferences, WTO document G/RO/W/191, 9 October 2019.

10 See G/RO/W/187/Rev.1 Impact of Direct Consignment Requirements on Preference Utilization by Least Developed Countries, October 2019.

3. Recent Developments and Challenges on Identifying Best Practices on Operational Certification Procedures

During the implementation of the GSP rules of origin, the traditional format and elements of OCPs contained in Annex K of the RKC were further developed and made operational: (1) the definition and content of rules of origin, (2) documentary evidence of origin, and (3) control of documentary evidence of origin.

Intergovernmental deliberations in the UNCTAD Special Committee on Preferences and related discussions on origin issues for the implementation of GSP and its rules of origin led to the adoption of the first multilaterally agreed model of certificate of origin (Form A) at UNCTAD.[11]

As FTA negotiations substantially increased in the past few decades, the traditional OCP format migrated progressively from a focus on unilateral trade preferences granted under GSP to more sophisticated and complete OCPs contained in FTAs. Most of the first-generation FTAs adopted the GSP model of a certificate of origin stamped by a certifying authority, mostly a ministry of trade or customs.[12]

The ASEAN Free Trade Area adopted such a model as many other preferential trading arrangements when it came into force in 1992.

Since the early days of GSP, the US and Canada marked a distinction from the reliance on certifying authorities. Since the late 1970s, while recognizing that proof of origin could be provided by a GSP Form A, both the US and Canada have not required the GSP Form A to have been stamped and signed by certifying authorities.

The flourishing of FTAs in the last decades, accompanied by (1) lack of a multilateral model/best practice of OCPs and (2) the emergence of information technology (IT) solutions to replace the hard-copy (paper) certificate of origin, has given rise to a variety of different models of OCPs.

The absence of multilateral disciplines on OCPs and the increased proliferation of FTAs have generated complexities in managing the growing numbers of different OCPs contained in FTAs. This has pushed governments to find trade-facilitating solutions. Unfortunately, the lack of an intergovernmental fora where experiences and best practices on OCPs can be exchanged has nurtured different school of thoughts on the best way to manage OCPs, including their variations.[13]

The main methodologies available to manage OCP are summarized in Table 1.

11 For a thorough review of the work carried out by UNCTAD working groups on rules of origin, see Inama (2022).

12 Japan also recognized chambers of commerce in beneficiary countries as certifying authorities under the GSP.

13 Recent meetings of the Technical Committee on Rules of Origin at the World Customs Organization (WCO) initiated discussion on the different options of digital solutions to manage e-COs.

Table 1: Main Methodologies Used Worldwide to Prove Origin of Goods

Main methodologies of proof of origin		Examples and comments
1.	**Certifying authority**	This method of proof of origin is based on a certifying authority, normally a public body such customs, a ministry of trade, or single-window that delivers the proof of origin: a hard-copy or an electronic certificate of origin (e-CO).
a)	Certificate of origin stamped and signed by certifying authorities	This is the most traditional, if not archaic, method to manage proof of origin based on the exchange of stamps and signatures. Despite the rapid evolution of alternatives, this method is still in use in the majority of ASEAN+1 free trade agreements (FTAs), the Regional Comprehensive Economic Partnership (RCEP), and the Comprehensive and Progressive Agreement for Trans-Pacific Partnership (CPTPP) for some member states. A variant was introduced by the European Union (EU) that does not require the exchange of specimen of signatures
b)	E-COs	E-COs are routinely issued by the International Chamber of Commerce (ICC) for non-preferential rules of origin.[a] In addition there is a proliferation of initiative in FTAs to establish electronic certificates of origin to different degrees of sophistication. In any case, the e-CO is delivered by a certifying authority.
c)	E-COs via ASEAN Single Windows	E-COs exchanged through the ASEAN Single Window for the ASEAN Trade in Goods Agreement (ATIGA) and increasingly other bilateral FTAs at the initiative of various ASEAN member states.
2)	**Self-certification**	This method of proof of origin is based on the principle that the individual, being a producer, exporter, or importer, self-certify the origin of the goods. Several variants of self-certification are listed below.
a)	Statement of origin by approved exporters	Under the approved exporter method, the certifying authority delegates to approved exporters who meet a series of criteria the authority to self-certify origin through a declaration or statement of origin. This method is used by some EU–ASEAN FTAs, RCEP, CPTPP (Under Annex 3A), and in the ASEAN-wide Self-Certification process.[b]
b)	Statement of origin by registered exporters	Registered exporter is a relatively new method to administer proof of origin. It has been introduced by the EU[c] in the context of the EU GSP and is progressively used in some EU FTAs with Asian countries such as Japan, Singapore, and Viet Nam.
c)	Certificate of origin signed by any exporter	This is one of the most liberal methods to administer proof of origin since any exporter may certify the origin of the goods. It is expected to become the main method in several Asian FTAs, but is not yet in force as discussed in Sections 4.2 to 4.4.
d)	Importer declaration	The importer declaration has been used mainly by the United States, which has consistently refrained from accepting certificates of origin or other forms of certification issued by exporters or certifying authorities. Japan recently introduced the importer declaration in the Japan–EU FTA and RCEP. CPTPP uses importer declaration as standard method of proof of origin, albeit transitional periods are allowed. This option is discussed in Sections 4.2 to 4.4.

[a] See ICC. Certificates of Origin. https://iccwbo.org/world-chambers-federation/chamber-services/certificates-of-origin/#anchor-cos-digitalisation.

[b] See the *ASEAN-wide Self-Certification (AWSC) Guidebook*, ASEAN Secretariat, Jakarta, December 2020. The People's Republic of China(PRC) has introduced a new concept of approved exporter as discussed in Section 4.2

[c] See https://taxation-customs.ec.europa.eu/online-services/online-services-and-databases-customs/rex-registered-exporter-system_ene.

Source: Compiled by the authors.

As outlined in Table 1, the main difference among the different forms of proof of origin relates to the role played by certifying authorities, in most cases government authorities (i.e., customs departments or trade ministries) issue proof of origin and manage OCPs.

The certifying authorities oversee issuing and certifying the certificate of origin (CO). This certification procedure may be exercised by different modalities such as:

(a) requiring to bring hard (in paper) evidence of compliance with rules of origin to issue a hard-copy CO to be stamped and signed by the competent certifying authority;

(b) by introducing in a portal, the required soft copy documentation to allow the issuance of a hard-copy certificate of origin or a soft-copy e-CO; and

(c) by delivering a certificate of origin in hard copy that can be transformed into a PDF document to be sent electronically (by email) to the importer;

(d) by introducing in a portal (ASEAN single window) evidence of compliance with rules of origin to issue an e-CO that is transmitted to the corresponding ASEAN single window of destination member country.

The diversity of the role played by the certifiying authorities in issuing COs or e-COs, and the corresponding acceptance by the importing certifying authorities is made increasingly complex by many countries in Asia and the Pacific undertaking bilateral initiatives to cover the legal implication of accepting various e-CO forms. Mega-regional FTAs such as RCEP and CPTPP do not create a common platform as both allow long transitional periods and many options before the adoption of a common regime.

Box 1: Unilateral and/or Bilateral Initiatives of Electronic Certificates of Origin in Asia and the Pacific

In December 2023, the Viet Nam's Ministry of Industry and Trade, acting as the certifying authority, unilaterally announced[a] that from 1 January 2024, it would issue, sign, and stamp certificates of origin (COs) electronically for nearly all free trade agreements (FTAs).[b] Accordingly, an exporter in Viet Nam can now send an electronic CO (e-CO) to the importer to print that e-CO on paper in ISO-standard format, with a specific QR code for verification. In practice, this type of 'EcoSys' is aimed at facilitating the application and issuance of the CO form since all steps or procedures are done electronically. However, some countries raised concerns over the legal basis in the Association of Southeast Asian Nations' FTAs with dialogue partners (ASEAN+1 FTAs). Ultimately, Viet Nam had to reintroduce the certificate of origin Form AI in hard copy.

Notes:
[a] See: https://lawnet.vn/vb/Thong-bao-1089-TB-XNK-2023-cap-Giay-chung-nhan-xuat-xu-hang-hoa-mau-E-AI-AJ-AANZ-AHK-90966.html.
[b] With the exclusion of EVFTA, UKVFTA, VN-EAEU.
Source: Authors' findings.

Certifying authorities have increasingly developed what are known as Electronic Origin Data Exchange Systems (EODES) like Korea FTAPASS[14] or the ASEAN Single Window. As discussed further, under these IT systems, the user can access a website to upload electronically the necessary documents needed for issuance of a CO that will be electronically transmitted to the importing partner authority. In addition, the Korean FTAPASS provides a series of additional services and advice for firms.

[14] See https://ftapass.or.kr/site/english/page/register/viewBasic.do.

In parallel to methods based on certifying authorities managing proof of origin, countries in Asia and the Pacific have introduced various forms of self-certification in FTAs. Presently, there is a wide variety of self-certification methods contained in different FTAs such as:

(a) approved exporters; or
(b) registered exporters; or
(c) any producer, exporter, or importer.

Several variations relate to how the self-certification can be made:

(a) prescribed statement on the commercial invoice,
(b) minimum information requirements, or
(c) any other document.

For instance, CPTPP adopted the self-certification principle based on what is defined as minimum information requirements,[15] even with a series of transitional periods for several contracting parties.

The importer-based declaration is another example of self-certification where the importer makes the original declaration at the time of customs clearance. It is the preferred option under CPTPP, albeit with a long transitional implementation period.

While there are pros and cons in each of the method that may be used to prove origin, series of lessons learned and best practices should be considered when discussing the differences among methods of proof of origin based on certifying authorities and methods of proof of origin based on self-certification.

On one hand, various IT solutions are branded as the most trade-facilitating options to manage proof of origin and OCPs. On the other hand, self-certification is championed as the easiest and best solution, with the added benefit of no additional costs involved.

The WCO Guidelines on Certification of Origin (July 2014, updated June 2018) are clear on this aspect, pointing to self-certification as the best option:

"Guideline: (FOSTERING THE USE OF SELF-CERTIFICATION OF ORIGIN) Considering the increasing volume of preferential trade and recognizing the need for the facilitation of origin-related procedures, self-certification of origin by a producer, manufacturer, exporter and/or importer shall be utilized to the maximum extent possible while recognizing the specificities of domestic business environment."

Yet, it has to be recognized that many countries are reluctant to move toward self-certification. ASEAN has been moving from pilot projects to promote self-certification to the ASEAN-wide self-certification to e-COs via the ASEAN Single Window as discussed further in Section 6.

Figure 1 portrays the differences between the traditional method of proof of origin administration when COs are paper-based and when they are digitalized. Comparison reveals that aside from the increased speed resulting from digitalization, the procedures and the number of steps undertaken in an EODES transaction are much the same as those in the issuance and exchange of paper-based COs. In addition,

[15] The CPTPP does not have a prescribed format for a CO. A CO for the CPTPP can be provided on an invoice or any other document (in either hard copy or electronic format), but it must contain a set of minimum data requirements set out in Annex 3B of Chapter 3 of the agreement

Figure 1: Certifying Authority Aministration of Proof of Origin versus Digitalization (EODES)

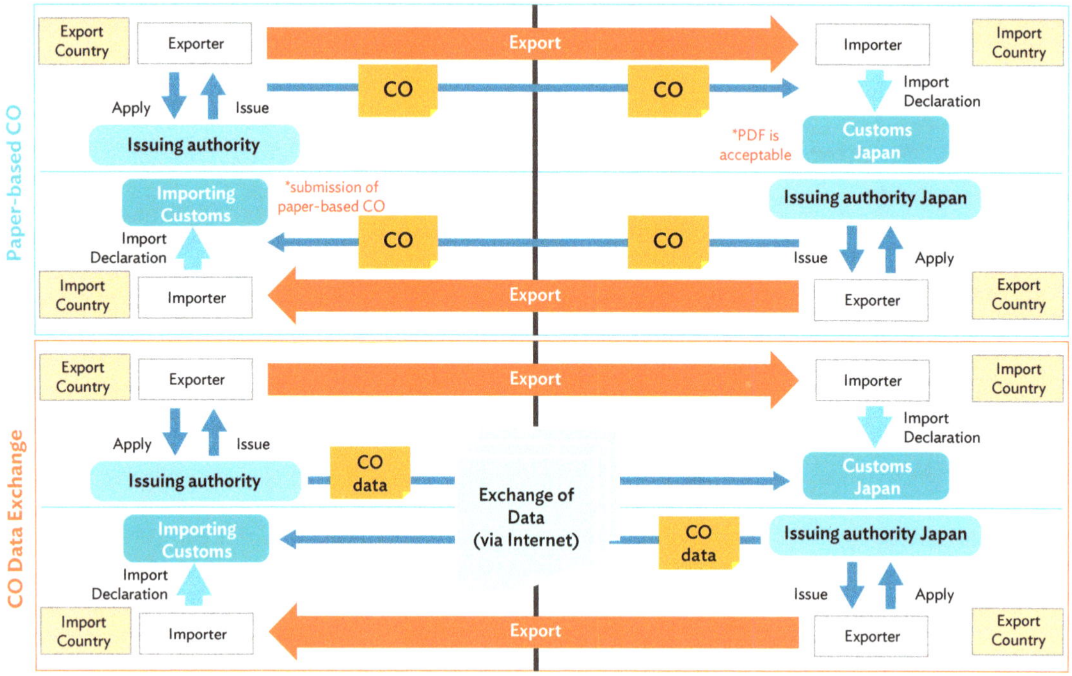

CO = certificate of origin, EODES = Electronic Origin Data Exchange Systems.
Source: Excerpted and adapted from a presentation at the World Customs Organization 3rd Global conference by Mariko Haga of the International Cooperation Division Customs and Tariff Bureau, Ministry of Finance, Japan, 8 November 2023.

during the implementation phase of an EODES system, elaboration of the specifications for the exchange of CO data may take time, requiring mutual agreements and a tested, shared IT environment.

ASEAN has embraced the electronic route with e-CO Form D exchanged through the ASEAN Single Window that became officially operational in January 2024.[16]

Under the ASEAN Single Window, the e-CO Form D has digitalized paper-based COs and linked CAs to the ASEAN national single windows. Yet the role of certifying authorities in validating the information and documentation provided by the exporter remains the same as shown in Figure 1.

RCEP adopts the traditional way of OCPs in ASEAN FTAs creating another layer of OPCs and CO. Yet RCEP provides for a built-in agenda to move to more trade-facilitating practices of OPCs, including self-certification.

In short, the region is divided on the best solutions to manage proof of origin and OPCs. The next section aims to identify the differences in solutions, present the possible best practices, and then chart a way forward.

[16] See https://asean.org/wp-content/uploads/2024/01/Full-Implementation-of-e-Form-D-Final.pdf. Yet reports indicate that implementation of the Lao People's Democratic Republic e-CO has been delayed.

4. Different Forms of Proof of Origin in ATIGA, ASEAN+1, and Selected Asian Free Trade Agreements

Depicting the various forms of proof of origin and OCPs in ATIGA, ASEAN+1, and in the two Asian megaregional agreements, the CPTPP[17] and RCEP, is like hitting a moving target and a major goal of this study.

In a characteristic ASEAN way, for ATIGA and for each ASEAN+1 FTA, there is a proliferation of legal texts and annexes related to proof of origin and OCPs that need to be reconciled. Also, countries in Asia and the Pacific have a wide disparity of views about the most appropriate methods of managing proof of origin and OCPs. The range is reflected in the two mega-regional agreements, the CPTPP and RCEP, providing different methods for proof of origin and OCP among parties, while different timetables create another layer of complication.

Lastly, individual countries in Asia and the Pacific are progressively introducing unilateral measures related to proof of origin and OCPs, or negotiating bilateral arrangements in the context of ASEAN+1 FTAs or bilateral FTAs.[18] Some CPTPP members have introduced a CO template even as the agreement does not provide for a CO, while, as shown in Box 1, Viet Nam has unilaterally introduced an e-CO in the sense that it is delivered electronically by the country's issuing authority.

This section analyses the different proof of origin and OCPs used in ATIGA, ASEAN+1 FTAs, RCEP, and CPTPP. The objective is to identify deviations from a common pattern that should have informed the negotiating process of OCPs with a series of FTA with dialogue partners. Similarly, RCEP and CPTPP were expected to serve as unifying platform to put a lid on the Pandora's Box of different PSROs and OCP, which have proliferated across each new FTA established in Asia and the Pacific over the past few decades.

The analysis covers the three main conditions to comply with the substance and procedural aspects of rules of origin common to all FTAs. First, the goods must comply with the rules of origin requirement under the applicable across-the-board criterion or the PSRO under the FTA. Second, they must comply with consignment conditions (documentary evidence of direct consignment may be required). Third, the goods have to be accompanied by proof of origin or declared as originating in accordance with FTA procedures.

In addition, ancillary requirements that determine the granting of preferential treatment at the time of customs clearance will be contrasted. This will include, for instance, the retrospective issuance of proof of origin, third-country or third-party invoicing, back-to-back certificates of origin, and other requirements.

---

17 CPTPP is different from ASEAN +1 and RECP. In ASEAN+1 and RCEP, ASEAN negotiated as a bloc. This was not the case in CPTPP. Only four ASEAN member states (Brunei Darussalam, Malaysia, Singapore, and Viet Nam) are part of the CPTPP.

18 See Box 1 for an example: Viet Nam has unilaterally introduced an e-CO procedure.

4.1 Forms of Certificate of Origin in ATIGA, ASEAN+1, and RCEP

The CO forms in ASEAN FTAs process has had a long and troubled history, starting from the ASEAN Free Trade Area (AFTA) in 1992. AFTA Rule 7 at that time best summarizes the difficult start by providing specific standards and colors for Form D as follows:

"RULE 7: ISSUANCE OF CERTIFICATE OF ORIGIN

- *(a) The Certificate of Origin must be on ISO A4 size paper in conformity to the specimen as shown in Appendix "A". It shall be made in English.*
- *(b) The Certificate of Origin shall comprise one original and three (3) carbon copies of the following colours:*
- *(c) Original - light viole*
    - *Duplicate – orange*
    - *Triplicate – orange*
    - *Quadruplicate – orange*
- *(d) Each Certificate of Origin shall bear a reference number separately given by each place or office of issuance."*

It is therefore not surprising that early reports and studies on AFTA implementation found Form D rejected for trivial reasons such as the size of a CO was 1 or 2 millimeters too big or too small, e.g., as not being "A4" size; the paper was the wrong shade of color (e.g., for not being sufficiently "violet" or being too "light"); the signature was slightly different from the specimen signature (e.g., a dot was missing from an "i") or in a slightly different location from specimen signature); or the document used the wrong font type (Inama and Sim 2015). These initial difficulties remain a constant feature of AFTA and its successor ATIGA, as will be discussed.

Table 2 compares administrative requirements related to the issuance of COs by certifying authorities—under ATIGA, selected ASEAN FTAs, and RCEP. It shows the issuance modalities and whether notification to other ASEAN member states is required. CPTPP is not included since its importer-based method does not provide for COs issued by certifying authorities. CPTPP only allows certification by either certifying authorities or approved exporters upon notification from the CPTPP party to derogate from the importer-based method for an initial period of 5 years (and allows this to be extended for another 5 years).[19]

Table 2 makes it clear that ATIGA and ASEAN+1 FTAs have adopted as starting points the methodology based on a CO issued by certifying authorities with the exchange of seals and signatures of authorized certification officials.

[19] See paragraph 5 Annex 3A of CPTPP: An exporting Party may require that a certification of origin for a good exported from its territory be either: (a) issued by a competent authority or(b) completed by an approved exporter.

Table 2: Issuance of Certificates of Origin and Notification in ATIGA, ASEAN+1 Free Trade Agreements, and RCEP

Agreement	Certificate of origin issued by	Details to be provided
ATIGA	Issuing authority means the Government authority of the exporting Member State designated to issue a Certificate of Origin (Form D) and notified to all the other Member States in accordance with this Annex[a]	Each Member State shall provide a list of the names, addresses, specimen signatures, and specimen of official seals of its issuing authorities, in hard copy and soft copy format, through the ASEAN Secretariat for dissemination to other Member States in soft copy format. Any change in the said list shall be promptly provided in the same manner. The specimen signatures and official seals of the issuing authorities, compiled by the ASEAN Secretariat, shall be updated annually. Any Certificate of Origin (Form D) issued by an official not included in the list referred to in paragraph 1 shall not be honored by the receiving Member State.[b]
ACFTA	The Certificate of Origin (Form E) shall be issued by the Issuing Authorities of the exporting Party.[c]	A Party shall inform all the other Parties of the names and addresses of its respective Issuing Authorities and shall provide specimen signatures and specimen of official seals, and correction stamps, if any, used by its Issuing Authorities. The above information and specimens shall be provided to all the other Parties to the Agreement and a copy furnished to the ASEAN Secretariat. A Party shall promptly inform all the other Parties of any changes in names, addresses, or official seals in the same manner.[d]
AANZFTA[e]	The Certificate of Origin shall be issued by an Issuing Authority/ Body of the exporting Party. Details of the Issuing Authorities/ Bodies shall be notified by each Party, through the ASEAN Secretariat, prior to the entry into force of this Agreement. Any subsequent changes shall be promptly notified by each Party, through the ASEAN Secretariat.[f]	The Issuing Authorities/Bodies shall provide the names, addresses, specimen signatures, and specimens of the impressions of official seals of their respective Issuing Authorities/Bodies to the other Parties, through the ASEAN Secretariat. The Issuing Authorities/Bodies shall submit electronically to the ASEAN Secretariat the above information and specimens for dissemination to the other Parties. Any subsequent changes shall be promptly notified through the ASEAN Secretariat. Any Certificate of Origin issued by a person not included in the list may not be honored by the Customs Authority of the importing Party.[g]
AJCEP	The competent government authority of the exporting Party shall, upon request made in writing by the exporter or its authorized agent, issue a Certificate of Origin or, under the authorization given in accordance with the applicable laws and regulations of the exporting Party, may designate other entities or bodies (hereinafter referred to as "designees") to issue a Certificate of Origin.[h]	Each Party shall provide the other Parties with a list of names and addresses, and a list of specimen signatures and specimen of official seals or impressions of stamps for the issuance of a Certificate of Origin, of its competent government authority and, if any, its designees. Any Certificate of Origin bearing a signature not included in the list referred to in paragraph 2 shall not be valid.[i]

continued on the next page

Table 2 continued.

Agreement	Certificate of origin issued by	Details to be provided
AKFTA	Issuing authority means the competent authority designated by the government of the exporting Party to issue a Certificate of Origin and notified to all the other Parties in accordance with this Appendix.[j]	Each Party shall provide the names, addresses, specimen signatures, and specimen of official seals of its issuing authorities to all the other Parties, through the ASEAN Secretariat. Any change in the said list shall be promptly provided in the same manner.[k]
RCEP	A Certificate of Origin shall be issued by the issuing body of an exporting Party upon an application by an exporter, a producer, or their authorized representative. The exporter, producer, or their authorized representative shall apply in writing or by electronic means for a Certificate of Origin, to the issuing body of the exporting Party in accordance with the exporting Party's laws, regulations, and procedures.	Each Party shall provide the names, addresses, specimen signatures, and impressions of official seals of its issuing body to the other Parties. Such information shall be submitted electronically through the RCEP Secretariat established pursuant to subparagraph 1(i) of Article 18.3 (Functions of the RCEP Joint Committee) (hereinafter referred to as "RCEP Secretariat"), for dissemination to the other Parties. Any subsequent changes shall be promptly submitted to the RCEP Secretariat in the same manner for dissemination to the other Parties. The Parties shall endeavor to establish a secure website to display such information from the last 3 years, and such website shall be accessible to the Parties. Notwithstanding paragraph 6, a Party shall not be required to provide the specimen signatures of its issuing body to the RCEP Secretariat for dissemination to the other Parties if it has established its own secured website, containing relevant information of the Certificates of Origin it issues, including their Certificate of Origin numbers, HS Codes, descriptions of goods, quantities, dates of issuance, and names of the exporters, that is accessible to the Parties. The Parties shall review the requirement to provide specimen signatures of the issuing bodies 3 years after the date of entry into force of this Agreement for all signatory States.

AANZFTA = ASEAN-Australia-New Zealand Free Trade Area, ACFTA = ASEAN–China Free Trade Area, AJCEP = ASEAN–Japan Comprehensive Economic Partnership, AKFTA = ASEAN–Korea Free Trade, ASEAN = Association of Southeast Asian Nations, ATIGA = ASEAN Trade in Goods Agreement, RCEP = Regional Comprehensive Economic Partnership.

[a] ATIGA Annex 8 Rule 1. In addition, pilot programs for self-certification have been implemented, see: https://www.asean.org/storage/images/2015/October/outreach-document/Edited%20ROO%20Self%20Certification.pdf.
[b] ATIGA Annex 8 Rule 2.
[c] ACFTA Appendix A Attachment A Rule 2.
[d] ACFTA Appendix A Attachment A Rule 3.
[e] This text refers to the first ASEAN-Australia-New Zealand FTA (AANZFTA) legal text. For updates of AANZA, see Section 4.1.
[f] AANZFTA Appendix 2 Section B Rule 1.
[g] AANZFTA Appendix 2 Section B Rule 2.
[h] AJCEP Annex 2 Rule 2.
[i] AJCEP Annex 4 Rule 2.
[j] AKFTA Appendix 1 Rule 1.
[k] AKFTA Appendix 1 Rule 2.

Note: Adapted and updated from Crivelli, Inama, and Pearson. 2023. *An Assessment of Rules of Origin in RCEP and ASEAN+ 1 Free Trade Agreements*. Asian Development Bank.

Sources: The indicated free trade agreements.

In the case of ATIGA and the ASEAN-Australia-New Zealand Free Trade Area (AANZFTA), there have been significant changes mainly contained in the latest revision of ATIGA OCPs[20] that have introduced the ASEAN-wide self-certification and the e-Form D transmitted electronically through the ASEAN Single Window.[21]

The second protocol to amend the agreement establishing the AAANZFTA (hereafter, the second protocol) introduced, as a replacement to the traditional Form AANZFTA, a simplified CO based on a list of data requirements[22] to be contained in a certificate of origin in addition to the provisions for a declaration of origin made by approved exporters according to a list of minimum data requirements.[23] In addition, the second protocol introduced the notion of self-certification by any exporter or producer with the caveat that such self-certification should be implemented not later than 10 years for Australia, Brunei Darussalam, Indonesia, Malaysia, New Zealand, the Philippines, Singapore, Thailand, and Viet Nam, and not later than 20 years for Cambodia, the Lao People's Democratic Republic (Lao PDR), and, Myanmar, with a possibility of extension for another 10 years. In addition, paragraph 4 of Rule 1 of Annex 3A on OCPs provides that: "The Parties shall commence a review of this Rule on the date of entry into force of the Second Protocol for all Parties. This review will consider the introduction of Declaration of Origin by an importer as a Proof of Origin."

The OCP of the remaining ASEAN+1 FTAs—the ASEAN–China Free Trade Area [ACFTA], the ASEAN–Korea Free Trade Area [AKFTA], and the ASEAN–Japan Comprehensive Economic Partnership [AJCEP]— were also revised, without marking a significant departure from the methodology based on COs issued through the exchange of seals and signatures of authorized officials. In particular, ACFTA underwent two revisions of OCP and rules of origin in 2010 and in 2019.[24]

AKFTA OCPs underwent an extended revision in 2014 and a more limited one in 2015. Yet, the 2015 revision set a new standard as a footnote recognized that: "A printed format means a Certificate of Origin manually or electronically signed, stamped and issued directly by the issuing authorities of the exporting Party."[25] This opened the way to what can be defined as a primary form of an e-CO system—i.e., the CO form may be issued electronically by the certifying authority and exchanged accordingly, or the exporter may send a PDF version of the paper-based CO to the importer. However, as emerged during consultations with stakeholders, use of this primary form of e-CO was made subject, in some instances, to the signing of a memorandum of understanding concerning its application.

The system of CO based on the exchange of seals and signatures reflects the most traditional, if not archaic, methodology from the early days of the GSP. At that time, UNCTAD was the repository of stamps of seals and signatures that had to be routinely distributed to UNCTAD members' states missions in Geneva, and in turn transmitted to capitals and regional customs offices. It emerged rapidly that such a

20 OCPs for the rules origin under Chapter 3 as endorsed by the 35th ASEAN Free Trade Area (AFTA) Council Meeting of September 2021.

21 The ASEAN Single Window was established by the Protocol on the Legal Framework, signed on 4 September 2014 in Viet Nam.

22 See Rule 8 "Issuance of certificate of origin" and Annex 3A.1 of the second protocol to amend the agreement establishing the ASEAN-Australia-New Zealand Free Trade Area (AANZFTA).

23 See Annex 3A.2 of second Protocol to amend the agreement establishing the AANZFTA.

24 See https://www.enterprisesg.gov.sg/-/media/esg/files/non-financial-assistance/for-companies/free-trade-agreements/acfta/acfta_legal_text.pdf.

25 See https://www.enterprisesg.gov.sg/-/media/esg/files/non-financial-assistance/for-companies/free-trade-agreements/ASEAN-Korea-FTA/AKFTA_Third_Protocol_to_Amend_the_ASEAN_Korea_Trade_in_Goods_Agreement_2015.pdf.

system was not efficient as it caused several delays on transmission of the seals and signatures, entailing difficulties such that goods were stopped at time of customs clearance, awaiting transmission of the updated notified seal and signatures.

Discussions within the UNCTAD intergovernmental machinery at that time addressed this problem by suggesting that notification of seals and stamps should be done directly to the preference-giving country and not just through the UNCTAD secretariat. Thus, the UNCTAD secretariat route became complementary to the direct notifications made among preference-granting and preference-receiving countries. Further discussions revealed that one of the main difficulties emerged from the rapid turnover of officials designated to sign the GSP Form and the need to notify new signatures. To address these difficulties, some preference-giving countries, starting with the EU, requested to notify only the seals and not to request the exchange of signatures.

It seems that the ASEAN secretariat and member states have yet to acknowledge these lessons since the centrality of ASEAN secretariat in disseminating seals and signatures has been maintained even in the latest revision of OPCs of ATIGA in 2021. On the contrary, the latest revision of ATIGA of 2021[26] expanded its traditional role of custodian of the seals and signatures to add a position as custodian of the ASEAN-wide self-certification database,[27] where certified exporters are registered.

In the case of GSP Form A, progressively all main preference-giving countries started to adopt self-certification or adopted trade-facilitating practices (Japan adopting self-certification for certain products), and UNCTAD relinquished the role of disseminating seals and signature.

The difficulties reported from using a system based on exchange of seals and signatures in the face of the lessons learned through the evolution of the international trading system may appear somewhat overstated or out of proportion. However, even a more recent reading of excerpts from reports of the Sub-committee on ATIGA Rules of Origin (SCAROO), the body responsible for rules of origin in ASEAN, reveals complexities that have existed for decades. The management of proof of origin in ATIGA remains rooted into checking the form, particularly the documentary evidence, rather than verifying the actual origin of the goods.

A recent document emerging from the ASEAN intergovernmental machinery shows that in the 14 years from 2008 to 2022, no less than 38 intergovernmental meetings were held, involving 97 issues raised over the difficulties arising from ATIGA proof of origin and related OCPs.[28] Table 3 gives more detail on the issues that have repeatedly emerged.

A closer look at the issues raised at SCAROO shows that most of them were recurring issues regarding the fine details related to the certificate of origin Form D and associated OCPs, such as rules on the size of ticks in Form D and the verification of stamps and signatures. In addition, it seems that parallel forms of certification, including the co-existence of a paper-based Form D and an e-CO, have caused confusion (see Figure 2).

[26] See https://asean.org/wp-content/uploads/2021/09/ATIGA-08-Annex-8-Amended-OCP-endorsed-AFTAC35.pdf.

[27] See paragraph 5 of the OCPs for the rules origin under Chapter 3, as endorsed by the 35th AFTA Council Meeting in September 2021

[28] Excerpt from the SCAROO meeting of August 2022.

Figure 2: Recurrent Issues Discussed in Subcommittee on ATIGA Rules of Origin or Similar Meetings

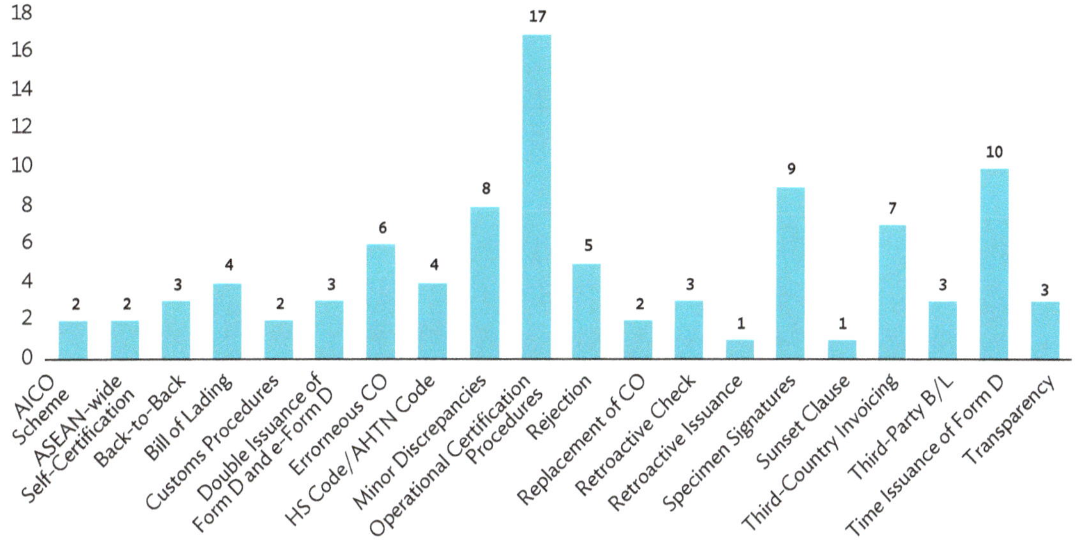

AICO = ASEAN industrial cooperation, ASEAN = Association of Southeast Asian Nations, ATIGA = ASEAN Trade in Goods Agreement, B/L = Bill of Lading, CO = certificate of origin, HS = Harmonized System, SCAROO = Subcommittee on ATIGA Rules of Origin.
Source: Authors, based on SCAROO documents.

The ATIGA intergovernmental machinery made significant progress toward transparency by posting on the internet a summary of issues raised in SCAROO and how they have been addressed. However, the succinct nature of the reports and the quality of their wording has significantly diminished their value since it is difficult to fully understand the issues raised and solutions found, if any.

The overall impression given by the SCAROO summary is that some of issues raised have persisted over the years and many more may emerge. There are no available reports of similar meetings concerning ASEAN+1 FTAs, even if the same method of proof of origin suggests that difficulties may be even more pronounced as the level of integration may not be as deep as in ASEAN.

Table 3 compares the different forms used in each ASEAN+1 FTA and RCEP. It is interesting that even with minor issues such as the number of copies, there is no apparent sign of efforts to rationalize, if not standardize, procedure related to how COs are issued in various ASEAN+1 FTAs.

Table 3: Certificates of Origin, Format and Distribution of Copies, ASEAN+1 FTAs, and RCEP

	ATIGA[a]	AANZFTA[b]	ACFTA[c]	AJCEP[d]	AKFTA[e]	RCEP[f]
Name of the form	Form D	Form AANZ	Form E	Form AJ	Form AK	Form RCEP
Specimen	Annex 7 of ATIGA	Attachment of AANZFT. Minimum data requirements in Appendix 2	Attachment Appendix 1 of 2015 Amendment to ACFTA	Attachment to Annex 4 of AJCEP, revised version published 2014	Attachment of AKFTA	As part of the implementation guidelines adopted by the RCEP joint Committee August 2022
Format	ISO A4 size white paper	Hardcopy; in English	ISO A4 size paper; in English	In English	A4 paper; in English	A4, English
Copies	1 original; 2 carbon copies	1 original; 2 copies	1 original; 2 copies	In the case of a Party which is an ASEAN Member State: 1 original, 2 copies. In the case of Japan: original only	1 original; 2 copies . The colors of the original and the copies shall be mutually agreed upon by the parties.	Not specified
Distribution of copies	Original forwarded by exporter to importer for the submission to customs authority. Duplicate retained by issuing authority. Triplicate retained by exporter.	Original be forwarded by exporter to importer for submission to the customs authority of the importing Party. Duplicate retained by the issuing authority. Triplicate retained by the exporter.	Original forwarded, by exporter to importer for submission to the customs authority Duplicate retained by issuing authority. Triplicate retained by exporter.	Original forwarded by the exporter to importer for submission to customs authority of importing Party. In the case of a Party which is an ASEAN Member State, a copy of the Certificate of Origin is to be retained by both the exporter and the competent governmental authority of the exporting Party or its designees, respectively.	Original forwarded by the producer and/or exporter to importer for submission to the customs authority of the importing Party. The duplicate retained by issuing authority of the exporting Party. The triplicate retained by producer and/ or exporter.	Not specified

AANZFTA = ASEAN-Australia-New Zealand Free Trade Area, ACFTA = ASEAN–China Free Trade Area, AJCEP = ASEAN–Japan Comprehensive Economic Partnership, AKFTA = ASEAN–Korea Free Trade, ATIGA = ASEAN Trade in Goods Agreement, RCEP = Regional Comprehensive Economic Partnership.

[a] Annex 8, http://investasean.asean.org/files/upload/Annex%208.pdf.
[b] Appendix 2, http://aanzfta.asean.org/wp-content/uploads/2017/02/AANZFTA-First-Protocol-Appendix-2B2.pdf.
[c] http://www.asean.org/storage/images/archive/documents/acfta/Appendix1-101125.pdf.
[d] http://www.mofa.go.jp/policy/economy/fta/asean/implement.pdf.
[e] Appendix, http://akfta.asean.org/uploads/docs/akfta-operational-certification-procedures.pdf.
[f] Appendix, http://akfta.asean.org/uploads/docs/akfta-operational-certification-procedures.pdf.

Source: Adapted and updated from Crivelli, Inama, and Pearson. 2023. *An Assessment of Rules of Origin in RCEP and ASEAN+1 Free Trade Agreements*. Asian Development Bank.

Each ASEAN+1 FTA provides for a different number and distribution of copies, and they also differ in nature and color. The move to different e-CO methods, especially in ATIGA, or to self-certification, may have considerably eased such requirements. It is worth noting that for many ASEAN+1 FTAs the hard-copy certificate of origin is still required. As example, the latest revision of ACFTA made in 2019 was based on the CO form with a series of strict definitions that echoed the AFTA of 1992 as follows:[29]

"Rule 8 ISSUANCE OF CERTIFICATE OF ORIGIN (FORM E)

a) The Certificate of Origin (Form E) must be on ISO A4 size white paper in conformity to the specimen shown in Appendix 1 of this OCP. It shall be filled out in English. The Certificate of Origin (Form E)shall comprise one (1) original and two (2) copies, namely, the duplicate and triplicate copies."

ACFTA is being updated and it is hoped that more trade-facilitating methods can be agreed.

In a similar fashion, other ASEAN member states have shown reservations in embracing self-certification. In spite of a provision in the EU–Viet Nam FTA allowing the adoption a system of registered exporters, Viet Nam has yet to implement it. And since Viet Nam has very few approved exporters because the approval process is complex and lengthy, the hard copy of Form EUR I is the most-used CO for exports from Viet Nam to the EU. Form EUR I is relatively straightforward and can be completed without the complexities of the ATIGA Form D, given that it does not contain comparable boxes 8 and 13. Yet, the color and quality of the paper standard required has created difficulties.[30] It has to be noted that in the other direction of trade, from the EU to Viet Nam, the EU has taken advantage of the provisions in the EU–Viet Nam FTA to introduce the use of Registered Exporter (REX). Thus, the same FTA applies different methods of proof of origin, depending on the direction of trade.

The reservations of member states regarding the acceptance of self-certification has been reported in several ways and is ultimately reflected in the outcome of FTA negotiations. During negotiations for the Malaysia-New Zealand FTA, Malaysia was insistent on adopting the option of a CO issued by an authorized or government body. New Zealand 's position was that self-certification of origin based on invoice declaration would be sufficient. The outcome was similar to the the EU–Viet Nam FTA situation: New Zealand exporters would provide self-issued invoice declarations, and Malaysian exporters would apply for a CO which New Zealand has little interest in looking at.

As earlier pointed out, OCP implementation issues in ATIGA and ASEAN+1 FTAs have been reported. ATIGA and other ASEAN+1 FTAs provide that when there is an alternative in a PSRO between Regional Value Content (RVC) and Change in Tariff Classification (CTC), the exporter may choose the method as provided in Rule 28 of ATIGA as follows:

"1. (a) *For the purposes of Article 26(b), goods shall be deemed to be originating in the Member State where working or processing of the goods has taken place:*

(i) *if the goods have a regional value content (hereinafter referred to as "ASEAN Value Content" or the "Regional Value Content (RVC)") of not less than forty percent (40%) calculated using the formula set out in Article 29; or*

[29] Available at https://www.enterprisesg.gov.sg/-/media/esg/files/non-financial-assistance/for-companies/free-trade-agreements/ASEAN-China-FTA/upgrade-protocol/Attachment-A-Revised-OCP.pdf.

[30] Interview with motorbike industry representatives in Viet Nam, November 2023.

(ii) *if all non-originating materials used in the production of the goods have undergone a change in tariff classification (hereinafter referred to as "CTC") at four-digit level (i.e., a change in tariff heading) of the Harmonized System."*

(b) *Each Member State shall permit the exporter of the good to decide whether to use paragraph 1 (a)(i) or 1(a)(ii) of this Article when determining whether the goods qualify as originating goods of the Member State.*

2. (a) *Notwithstanding paragraph 1 of this Article, goods listed in Annex 3 shall qualify as originating goods if the goods satisfy the product specific rules set out therein.*

(b) *Each Member State shall permit the exporter of the good to decide whether to use paragraph 1 (a)(i) or 1(a)(ii) of this Article when determining whether the goods qualify as originating goods of the Member State."*

In spite of this clear legal provision in subparagraph 1(b) and repeated in subparagraph 2(b), in some ASEAN countries when an exporter chooses to use CTC rules, the application process for proof of origin requires RVC/costing data before an exporter can submit CTC data. This practice is not only illegal but is also the exact opposite of the very principle of trade facilitation:

(a) Requiring RVC data negates the advantages of CTC that provide administrative simplicity with respect to RVC as CTC removes the accounting calculations and foreign exchange fluctuations.

(b) Noting that PSRO in ATIGA, ASEAN+1 FTAs, and ultimately RCEP are predominantly RVC or CTC, this is a real stumbling block.

(c) A ruling based on RVC/costing data increases business risk if a material cost changes. This is particularly so with commodity-based products or when foreign exchange fluctuations occur. A ruling based on CTC rules is more stable and reduces risk. These sentiments have been echoed in the Viet Nam survey discussed in Section 8, where 68% of more than 200 firms said they preferred CTC and only 11% opted for RVC.

4.1.1. Content of Certificates of Origin in ATIGA, ASEAN+1, and RCEP

As discussed in Section 2, the Annex K of the Revised Kyoto Convention (RKC) includes a CO template with nine boxes to be filled. GSP Form A, the only multilaterally agreed CO form used commercially, contains 12 boxes and may be considered a standard. Form D of ATIGA has 13, and the new RCEP form contains 17 boxes. From a trade facilitation standpoint, the fewer the boxes, the easier to fill out the form. The more boxes and "tick" entries needed for completing the CO, the more complicated, tedious, and prone to error the task becomes. Comparative analysis of the different forms used in ASEAN+1 FTAs shows that while the number of boxes remains at 13 boxes, the content of entries required for completion varies. In the ATIGA box 13, up to 7 different ticks may be selected depending on the different OCPs.

By way of example, Figure 3 shows the ATIGA Certificate of Origin (Form D).

Figure 3: Specimen Certificate of Origin for ATIGA (Form D)

1. Goods consigned from (Exporter's business name, address, country)

2. Goods consigned to (Consignee's name, address, country)

Reference No.

ASEAN TRADE IN GOODS AGREEMENT/ ASEAN INDUSTRIAL COOPERATION SCHEME CERTIFICATE OF ORIGIN

(Combined Declaration and Certificate)

FORM D

Issued in ____________ (Country)

See Overleaf Notes

3. Means of transport and route (as far as known)

Departure date

Vessel's name/Aircraft eto.

Port of Discharge

4. For Official Use

Preferential Treatment Given Under ASEAN Trade in Goods Agreement

Preferential Treatment Given Under ASEAN Industrial Cooperation Scheme

Preferential Treatment Not Given (Please state reason/s)

Signature of Authorised Signatory of the Importing Country

5. Item number	6. Marks and numbers on packages	7. Number and type of packages, description of goods (including quantity where appropriate and HS number of the importing country)	8. Origin criterion (see Overleaf Notes)	9. Gross weight or other quantity and value (FOB)	10. Number and date of invoices

11. Declaration by the exporter

The undersigned hereby declares that the above details and statement are correct; that all the goods were produced in

____________ (Country)

and that they comply with the origin requirements specified for these goods in the ASEAN Trade in Goods Agreement for the goods exported to

____________ (Importing Country)

____________ Place and date, signature of authorised signatory

12. Certification

It is hereby certified, on the basis of control carried out, that the declaration by the exporter is correct.

____________ Place and date, signature and stamp of certifying authority

13.

☐ Third Country Invoicing	☐ Exhibition
☐ Accumulation	☐ De Minimis
☐ Back-to-Back CO	☐ Issued Retroactively
☐ Partial Cumulation	

Notes: Box 1 must contain the exporter details. The name, address and country of the exporter must be identified to specify from where the goods are consigned. To indicate where goods are sent to, box 2 has to be filled with the consignee's name, address and country. As far as is known, the shipment details, including the departure date, vessel name/aircraft, and the like, as well as port of discharge, must be given in box 3.

Box 4 must contain the signature of the authorized signatory of the importing country. Whether preferential treatment is accorded under the specific agreement must be indicated in box 4. The item number must be inserted in box 5 and the marks and numbers on packages detailed in box 6.

The number and type of packages, and a description of the goods, must be included in box 7. The HS number (of the importing Party) and quantity must be included where appropriate. The description of products must be sufficiently detailed to enable the products to be identified by the customs officers examining them. The name of the manufacturer and any trademark must also be specified. AANZFTA and AJCEP require indication at a six-digit level.*

Box 8 concerns the relevant origin-conferring criteria and is one of the most important and complicated boxes to be filled in. An exporter must indicate the original criteria met, according to the requirements in the relevant FTA. The gross weight or other quantity and value (free on board) must be indicated in box 9. Box 10 is for the number as well as the date of the invoices. In box 11, the exporter (including manufacturer or producer) must declare that the goods comply with the relevant origin requirements, and provide the place, date and signature of the authorized signatory. If after reviewing the supporting documentation the issuing authority is satisfied that the goods qualify for preferential treatment, it certifies in box 12 that the exporter's declaration is correct by providing its signature and stamp and indicating the place and date. Box 13 provides a number of options which may be ticked depending on their relevance to the particular certificate of origin.

* AJCEP: With respect to subheading 2208.90 and 9404.90, in an exceptional case where the good is a specific product requiring a special description (for example, "sake compound and cooking sake (Mirin) of subheading 2208.90", "beverages with a basis of fruit, of an alcoholic strength by volume of less than 1 per cent of subheading 2208.90", "quilts and eiderdowns of 9404.90") such description of specific products should be indicated.

AANZFTA = ASEAN-Australia-New Zealand Free Trade Area, AJCEP = ASEAN–Japan Comprehensive Economic. Partnership, ATIGA = ASEAN Trade in Goods Agreement, FOB = free on board, FTA = free trade agreement, HS = Harmonized System.
Source: ATIGA, Annex 7; and UNCTAD. 2021. *Handbook on preferential market access for ASEAN least developed countries (Part III).*

Table 4 shows how the entries in box 8 of each ASEAN+1 FTA and RCEP should be made.

Table 4: Origin Criteria: Entries Required in Box 8

	ATIGA	AANZFTA	AIFTA	ACFTA	AJCEP	AKFTA	RCEP
Goods wholly obtained or produced (WO)	WO	WO	WO	WO	WO	WO	WO
Goods entirely produced (PE)	Not included	PE	Not included	Not included	PE	Not included	PE
Regional value content (RVC)	Percentage of regional value content, e.g., 40%	RVC	Not included	Percentage of single-country content,[a] e.g., 40%. Percentage of ACFTA cumulative content,[b] e.g., 40%	RVC	RVC 40%	RVC
Change in tariff classification (CTC)	The actual CTC rule, e.g., CC, CTH or CTSH	CTC, whether on chapter, heading, or subheading level, no need to place actual tariff shift	Not included	Not included	CTC	CTH	CTC
Specific processes (SP)	SP	Not included	Not included	Not included	SP	Specific Processes	Chemical Reaction (CR)
Combination criteria	Actual combination criterion, e.g., CTSH + 35%	CTSH + RVC, actual PSE needs to be inserted	RVC [ ] percent + CTSH	Not included	CTH or RVC	CTH or RVC 40%	Not included
Product-specific requirement (PSR)	Not included	"Other" for PSR included in Annex 2	Appropriate qualifying criteria	PSR	Not included	CTC WO-AK[c] RVC, e.g., RVC 45% Combination rule that needs to be met for good to qualify as originating, e.g., CTH + RVC 40% Specific processes Rule 6[d]	Not included

continued on the next page

Table 4 continued.

	ATIGA	AANZFTA	AIFTA	ACFTA	AJCEP	AKFTA	RCEP
Partial cumulation (PC)	PC X percent, where X would be the percentage of regional value content of less than 40%, e.g., PC 25%	Not included	Not included	Not included	Not included	Not included	ACU
De minimis Accumulation (DMI ACU)	Not included	Not included	Not included	Not included	DMI ACU	Not included	DMI

AANZFTA = ASEAN-Australia-New Zealand Free Trade Area, ACFTA = ASEAN–China Free Trade Area, AIFTA = ASEAN–India Free Trade Area, AJCEP = ASEAN–Japan Comprehensive Economic Partnership, AKFTA = ASEAN–Korea Free Trade, ATIGA = ASEAN Trade in Goods Agreement, CC = Change in Chapter, CTH = Change in Tariff Heading, CTSH = Change in Tariff Subheading, DMI = de menemis, RCEP = Regional Comprehensive Economic Partnership.

Note: Adapted and updated from Crivelli, Inama, and Pearson. 2023. An assessment of Rules of Origin in RCEP and ASEAN+1 Free Trade Agreements.

[a] For the purpose of implementing the provisions of Rule 2 (b) of the ACFTA rules of origin, products worked on and processed as a result of which the total value of the materials, parts or produce originating from non-ACFTA member states or of undetermined origin used does not exceed 60% of the free-on-board value of the product produced or obtained and the final process of the manufacture is performed within the territory of the exporting Party.

[b] Products which comply with origin requirements provided for in rule 2 of the ACFTA rules of origin and which are used in a Party as inputs for a finished product eligible for preferential treatment in another/other Party/ Parties shall be considered as a product originating in the member state where working or processing of the finished product has taken place, provided that the aggregate ACFTA content of the final product is not less than 40%.

[c] Wholly obtained or produced in the territory of any Party.

[d] Goods satisfying rule 6.

Sources: Various free trade agreements.

Such extremely detailed prescriptions can be compared with GSP Form A, which also contained different entries for box 8 depending on the requirement of preference-giving countries. On one hand, GSP users routinely quoted box 8 as one of the most challenging issues. On the other hand, preference-giving countries took the view that since different GSP schemes have different rules of origin, the dedicated entries for box 8 were a safety issue to make sure that the GSP user correctly understood the RoO of the preference-giving country.

However, this reasoning is not applicable to ASEAN+1 FTAs in the sense that the Form and entries could have been negotiated by ASEAN and Dialogue partners based on a shared desire to adopt and rationalize standard entries to facilitate trade.

An example of best practice could have been drawn from Form EUR I, the standard used by the EU with FTAs partners. Even if the European FTAs contain different PSROs, Form EUR I does not contain a box 8 or an entry related to origin criteria.

If such a practice was not possible for ASEAN and its trade partners, then efforts could have been made to limit the deviations from a standard format, drawing inspiration for Canada CO forms under different FTAs (Table 5). As can be observed, deviation from the standard format is limited, the layout is almost identical, and the specific information required in the different entries is more limited in scope.

Table 5: Layout and Entries of Certificates of Origin in Canada FTAs

	Canada-Israel	Canada-Chile	Canada-Costa Rica	Canada-Peru	Canada-Jordan	Canada-Colombia	Canada-Republic of Panama	Canada-The Republic of Honduras	Canada-Republic of Korea
Number of Entries	10	11	12	13	11	12	10	13	11
HS Tariff Classification (Entry 6)	Yes	Yes	Yes	Yes	Yes	Yes	Yes	Yes	Yes
Preference Criterion (Entry 7)	Yes	Yes	Yes	Yes	Yes	Yes	Yes	Yes	Yes
Producer (Entry 8)	Yes	Yes	Yes	Yes	Yes	Yes	Yes	Yes	Yes
Value Test On RVC (Entry 9)	No	Yes	Yes	Yes	No	Yes	No	Yes	Yes
Country of Origin (Entry 10)	No	Yes	No	Yes	Yes (Entry 9)	Yes	No	Yes	Yes
Other	Yes. Gross weight or other quantity (Entry 9)	No	Yes. (Accu mulation, De minimis, Fungible goods and materials)	No	No	No	No	Yes. (Accu mulation, De minimis, Fungible goods and materials)	No

FTA = free trade agreement, HS = Harmonized System, RVC = regional value content.
Source: Canada FTAs.

Table 6 outlines the options for box 13 under ASEAN+1 FTAs and RCEP. This box's existence in addition to box 8 is another anomaly. The variation in entries required for different FTAs shows once again that when the FTAs were negotiated no attempt was made to establish a standard for the entries. In ATIGA, Box 13 has a special function related to cumulation. Form D can be used as the form for proving the origin of the goods that is going to be used for cumulation purposes. In short, Form D could be used as a kind of supplier declaration of origin when used to apply cumulation under ATIGA (article 30) as follows:

"Article 30 Accumulation

1. *Unless otherwise provided in this Agreement, goods originating in a Member State, which are used in another Member State as materials for finished goods eligible for preferential tariff treatment, shall be considered to be originating in the latter Member State where working or processing of the finished goods has taken place.*
2. *If the RVC of the material is less than forty percent (40%), the qualifying ASEAN Value Content to be cumulated using the RVC criterion shall be in direct proportion to the actual domestic content provided that it is equal to or more than twenty percent (20%). The Implementing Guidelines are set out in Annex 6."*

Table 6: Options to Tick Box 13 Under ASEAN+1 FTAs and RCEP

	ATIGA	AANZFTA	ACFTA	AJCEP	AKFTA	AHKFTA	RCEP
Third-country invoicing	X	X	X	X	X	X	X
Exhibition[a]	X		X		X	X	
Accumulation	X	X				X	
De minimis	X	X				X	
Back-to-back CO	X	X		X	X		X
Issued retroactively[b]	X	X		X		X	X
Partial cumulation	X						

AANZFTA = ASEAN-Australia-New Zealand Free Trade Area, ACFTA = ASEAN–China Free Trade Area, AHKFTA = ASEAN–Hong Kong, China Free Trade Agreement; AJCEP = ASEAN–Japan Comprehensive Economic Partnership, AKFTA = ASEAN–Korea Free Trade, ASEAN = Association of Southeast Asian Nations, ATIGA = ASEAN Trade in Goods Agreement, CO = certificate origin, RCEP = Regional Comprehensive Economic Partnership.

[a] In cases where goods are sent from the exporting member economies for exhibition in another economy and sold during or after the exhibition for importation into a member economy, indicate the name and address of the exhibition in Box 2.

[b] In exceptional cases, due to involuntary errors or omissions or other valid causes, the certificate of origin may be issued retroactively.

The practice of using a CO form for cumulation purposes, in this case Form D, is rather unique to ATIGA and has not been explicitly replicated in any other ASEAN+1 FTA.

Box 2: ATIGA Implementation Difficulties with Cumulation Provisions

A persistent implementation issue has been observed in the implementation of the Association of Southeast Asian Nations (ASEAN) Trade in Goods Agreement (ATIGA) provisions related to the allocation of origin when cumulation is used among different ASEAN Member States (AMS). Specifically, in the regional value content (RVC) 40 requirement, the example below illustrates a scenario where the requirement is met by cumulating processes in three member states. However, the last member refuses to issue a certficate of origin (CO) because its own local content represents "only" 5%.

Example: *a product complies with RVC requirement of 40%, with 35% of ingredients sourced from one ASEAN member state and the main manufacturing process* contributing an additional 20% RVC carried out in another member state. *The product is then sent as semi-finished good to a third member for finalization,* which adds 5% of RVC. *Despite the combined RVC meeting the 40% threshold, the third member is unwilling to issue CO Form D for exports to other member states due to its own "only" 5% local content. This approach defeats the concept of RVC.*

While provisions addressing this issue are contained in other free trade agreements, they are, at present, absent from ATIGA. Therefore, it would be advisable to insert a clear provision during the revision of ATIGA operational certification procedures to establish a methodology for identifying the originating ASEAN member state when cumulation is used.

Such clarification will help ensure that the RVC requirements are met and provide clarity to all stakeholders involved in the process. This is essential to prevent misinterpretation or misunderstandings that could result in rejections or delays in the Issuance of COs by the issuing authority in the final country of importation.

Source: Authors' own findings resulting from conversation with firms.

4.1.2 Back-to-Back Certificate of Origin

A back-to-back CO is a new CO issued by an intermediate exporting FTA partner country. It is based on the original CO issued by the first exporting FTA partner country. The back-to-back CO enables a company to ship its goods to an intermediate FTA partner country for trading or logistical purposes before re-exporting the goods to other FTA partner countries, while still retaining the origin status of the first exporting FTA partner country and the corresponding preferential tariff treatment of the goods.

The back-to-back CO is a common practice that has also been used in the context of EU FTAs, where it is called a replacement certificate.

Use of this OCP is rather self-explanatory in a world made of value chains relying on intermediate products stocked in different warehouses. However, the procedural requirements attached to this business reality may render it excessively costly or impracticable.

Figure 4: Back-to-Back Certificates of Origin

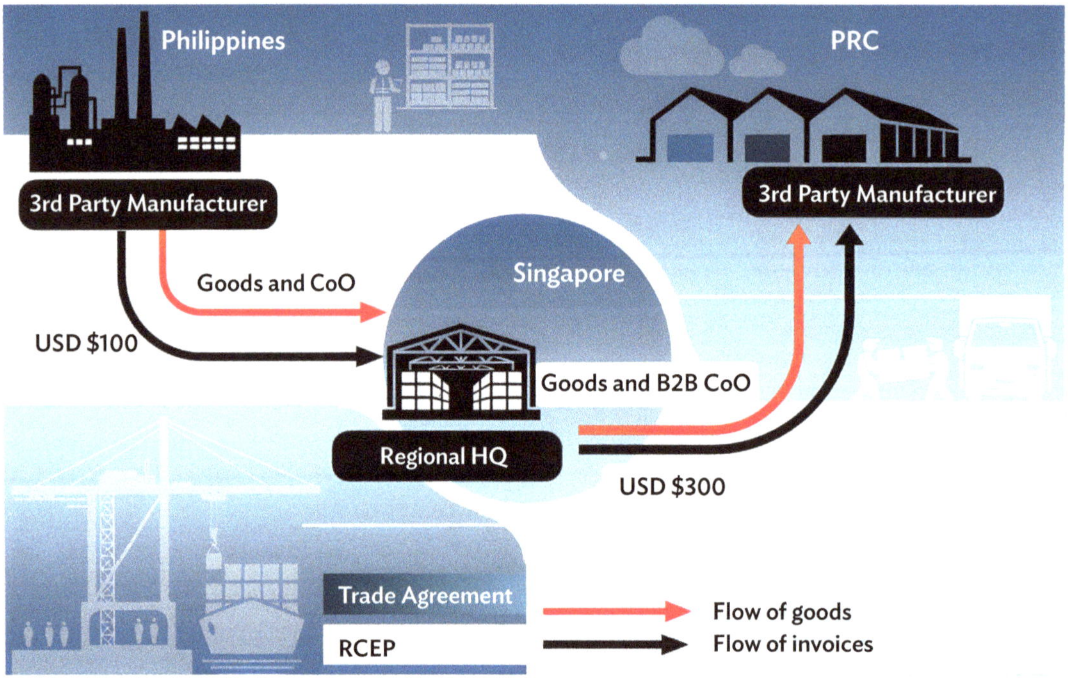

B2B = back-to-back, CoO = certificate of origin, HQ = headquarters, PRC = People's Republic of China, RCEP = Regional Comprehensive Economic Partnership,
Source: Elaboration from Anliker (2023).

Figure 4 shows the normal business practice where a manufacturer sells to the parent company located in another country and this company resells the goods with a markup price.

The exporter makes the application for a back-to-back CO. If the applicable conditions under the relevant FTA are met, the issuing authority of the intermediate party will agree to issue a back-to-back CO while the product is passing through that party's territory. Table 7 compares the conditions for the issuance of a back-to-back CO in the different FTAs.

Table 7: Comparison of Back-to-Back Certificate of Origin Conditions

ASEAN FTA	Rule/Article	Back-to-Back Certificate of Origin
ATIGA	Annex 8, Rule 10	Upon application by an exporter, the issuing authority of an intermediate Member State may issue a back-to-back CO if the following conditions are met. (a) A valid original CO (Form D) or certified true copy is presented. (b) The back-to-back CO issued contains some of the same information as the original CO. Every column in the back-to-back CO should be completed. (c) The FOB price of the intermediate Member State in Box 9 is reflected in the back-to-back CO. (d) For partial export shipments, the partial export value is shown instead of the full value of the original CO. The intermediate Member State will ensure that the total quantity re-exported under the partial shipment does not exceed the total quantity of the CO from the first Member State when approving the back-to-back CO to the exporters. (e) If information is not complete and/or circumvention is suspected, the final importing Member State(s) could request that the original CO is submitted to their respective customs authority. (f) Verification procedures (see Rules 18 and 19) are applied to the Member State issuing the back-to-back CO.
AANZFTA	Annex to Chapter 3 (Operational Certification Procedures), Rule 10(3)	An Issuing Authority/Body of an intermediate Party shall issue a back-to-back Certificate of Origin, if an application is made by the exporter while the good is passing through that intermediate Party, provided that: (i) A valid original CO or its certified true copy is presented. (ii) The period of validity of the back-to-back CO does not exceed the period of validity of the original CO. (iii) The consignment which is to be re-exported using the back-to-back CO does not undergo any further processing in the intermediate Party. Exceptions are repacking or logistics activities such as unloading, reloading, storing, or any other operations necessary to preserve them in good condition or to transport them to the importing Party. (iv) The back-to-back CO contains relevant information from the original CO in accordance with the minimum data requirements in Appendix 2 to the Annex on OCPs. (v) The FOB value is the FOB value of the goods exported from the intermediate Party. (vi) The verification procedures in Rules 17 and 18 of the Annex on OCPs also apply to the back-to-back CO.
ACFTA	N/A	ACFTA does not provide for back-to-back COs.
AJCEP	Annex 4, Rule 3(4)	An intermediate Party may issue a back-to-back CO upon request by the exporter in the importing Party or its authorized agent with presentation of the valid original CO. Where a valid back-to-back CO is issued, "an originating good of the exporting Party" shall be construed as an originating good of the Party whose competent governmental authority or its designees has issued the original CO.

continued on the next page

Table 7 continued.

ASEAN FTA	Rule/Article	Back-to-Back Certificate of Origin
AKFTA	Annex 3, Appendix 1, Rule 7	The issuing authority of the intermediate Party may issue a back-to-back CO, if an application is made by the exporter while the good is passing through its territory, if the following conditions are met. (a) A valid original CO is presented. (b) The importer of the intermediate Party and the exporter who applies for the back-to-back CO in the intermediate Party are the same. (c) Verification procedures as set out in Annex 3, Appendix 1, Rule 14, are applied.*
CPTPP	Not applicable	Not applicable
RCEP		1. Subject to Article 3.16 (Proof of Origin), an issuing body, approved exporter, or exporter of an intermediate Party may issue a back- to-back Proof of Origin provided that: (a) a valid original Proof of Origin or its certified true copy is presented; (b) the period of validity of the back-to-back Proof of Origin does not exceed the period of validity of the original Proof of Origin; (c) the back-to-back Proof of Origin contains relevant information from the original Proof of Origin in accordance with Annex 3B (Minimum Information Requirements); (d) the consignment which is to be re-exported using the back- to-back Proof of Origin does not undergo any further processing in the intermediate Party, except for repacking or logistics activities such as unloading, reloading, storing, splitting up of the consignment, or labelling only as required by the laws, regulations, procedures, administrative decisions, and policies of the importing Party, or any other operations necessary to preserve a good in good condition or to transport a good to the importing Party; (e) for partial export shipments, the partial export quantity shall be shown instead of the full quantity of the original Proof of Origin, and the total quantity re-exported under the partial shipment shall not exceed the total quantity of the original Proof of Origin; and (f) information on the back-to-back Proof of Origin includes the date of issuance and reference number of the original Proof of Origin. 2. The verification procedures referred to in Article 3.24 (Verification) shall also apply to the back-to-back Proof of Origin.

AANZFTA = ASEAN-Australia-New Zealand Free Trade Area, ACFTA = ASEAN–China Free Trade Area, AJCEP = ASEAN–Japan Comprehensive Economic Partnership, AKFTA = ASEAN–Korea Free Trade, ASEAN = Association of Southeast Asian Nations, ATIGA = ASEAN Trade in Goods Agreement, CCPTP = Comprehensive and Progressive Agreement for Trans-Pacific Partnership, CO = certificate origin, FOB = free on board, RCEP = Regional Comprehensive Economic Partnership.

* Note that the originating status of the goods can be retained for as long as 12 months with this specific arrangement; Original Form AK (6 months) plus Back-to-back Form AK (6 months). Available from: http://akfta.asean.org/uploads/docs/akfta-operational-certification-procedures.pdf, http://akfta.asean.org/uploads/docs/akfta-certificate-of-origin-form.pdf.

Sources: Free trade agreements legal texts.

As is apparent from Table 7, requirements for back-to-back CO procedures differ among FTAs. Some FTAs such as AKFTA require that the importer and exporter requesting the back-to-back CO are the same person. This puts an unnecessary limit to this OCP that otherwise is designed to allow flexibility in the management of COs. In addition, some FTAs describe in detail the operations that may be carried out on the goods while present in the intermediate country. Commercial reality militates for an ample interpretation of operations such as repackaging or logistical activities.

RCEP text regulates this issue quite exhaustively, whereas the silence of other FTAs on this issue may be interpreted differently, either that no operation may be carried out (which would be unreasonable) or that such operations are tolerated at the discretion of the certifying authority of the intermediary country.

As indicated in Table 2, issues related to back-to-back CO have been discussed in the ASEAN intergovernmental machinery dedicated to rules of origin and OCPs.

For instance, the November 2009 ASEAN meeting in Malaysia confirmed that the back-to-back CO Form D issued beyond the validity period of the original certificate could not be accepted. A back-to-back CO would need to be issued by the intermediate exporting member state and presented to the final importing member state within the validity period of the original certificate.

Linked to the issue of back-to-back CO is the requirement to provide documentary evidence related to direct shipment, as discussed at the ASEAN 2010 meeting in Hoi An, where the following was reported:

"Goods produced in Malaysia, sent to Viet Nam using multimodal transportation, e.g., by train to Singapore and by vessel to Viet Nam. In this case, there were two transportation documents, the first one issued to cover the transportation of the goods to Singapore, and a second B/L was be issued by a Singaporean company to ship the goods to Viet Nam."

The recommendation was to issue a single bill of lading (B/L) issued by the exporting country, describing all transportation modes required at the time of exportation. Commercially speaking, such a recommendation is quite stringent and revealing of the amount of scrutiny that direct shipment comes under in trade within ASEAN member states.

Box 3: Inconsistent Implementation of Back-to-Back Provisions and Related Difficulties in the ASEAN-Australia-New Zealand Free Trade Area

Certain practices within the Association of Southeast Asian Nations (ASEAN) appear to prohibit partial shipments for back-to-back certificates of origin. Additionally, requirements for non-manipulation certificates have been imposed for shipments transiting through non-AANZ (ASEAN-Australia-New Zealand) economies, particularly when transit occurs in the People's Republic of China; Hong Kong, China; or Taipei,China, to ensure that no additional processes or items are introduced during transit. These requirements have posed challenges, as exporters in Australia and New Zealand typically do not provide such certificates, leading to inconsistencies in the implementation of the ASEAN-Australia-New Zealand Free Trade Area (AANZFTA).

Source: Authors based on consultations with firms.

4.1.3 Third-Country and Third-Party Invoicing

Third-country invoicing is a common practice in today's international trade. It means that the exporter sells the goods to an intermediary that is reselling the goods to the final importer. Although the WCO guidelines recommend that this practice must be recognized (WCO 2018), the related procedures of ATIGA, ASEAN+1 FTAs, and RCEP are quite demanding and different.

Figures 5 and 6 illustrate such third-party invoicing schemes.[31]

Figure 5: Third-Party Invoicing with Three Parties

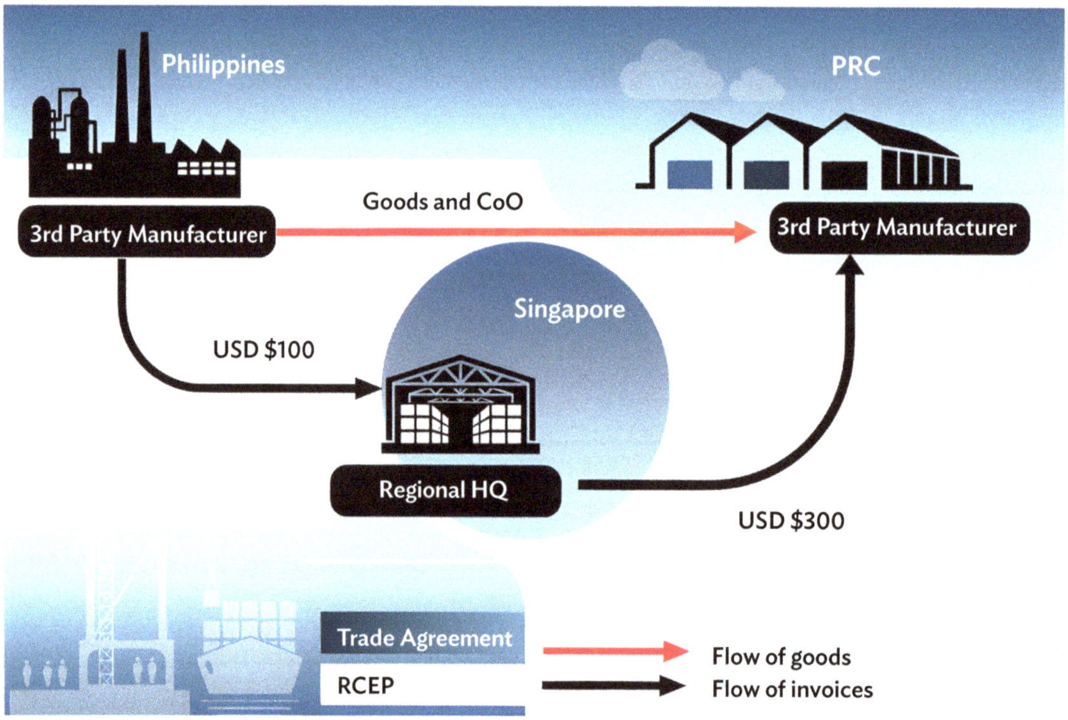

CoO = certificate of origin, HQ = headquarters, PRC = People's Republic of China, RCEP = Regional Comprehensive Economic Partnership.
Source: Elaboration from Anliker (2023).

In Figure 5, goods from the production facility in the Philippines are directly sold and shipped to the PRC, accompanied by a CO from the Philippines. However, the invoicing flow is going over [through] the headquarter in Singapore, adding a significant mark-up, and sold to the PRC for $300. The importing country will see a mismatch between a CO issued by Philippines and an invoice issued in Singapore and might be refusing the granting of preferential tariff treatment. A provision normally included in FTAs on third-country invoicing allows such practice subject to conditions that are now explained.

31 Note that "third party" in that context means "more than two."

Figure 6: Third-Party Invoicing with Four or More Parties

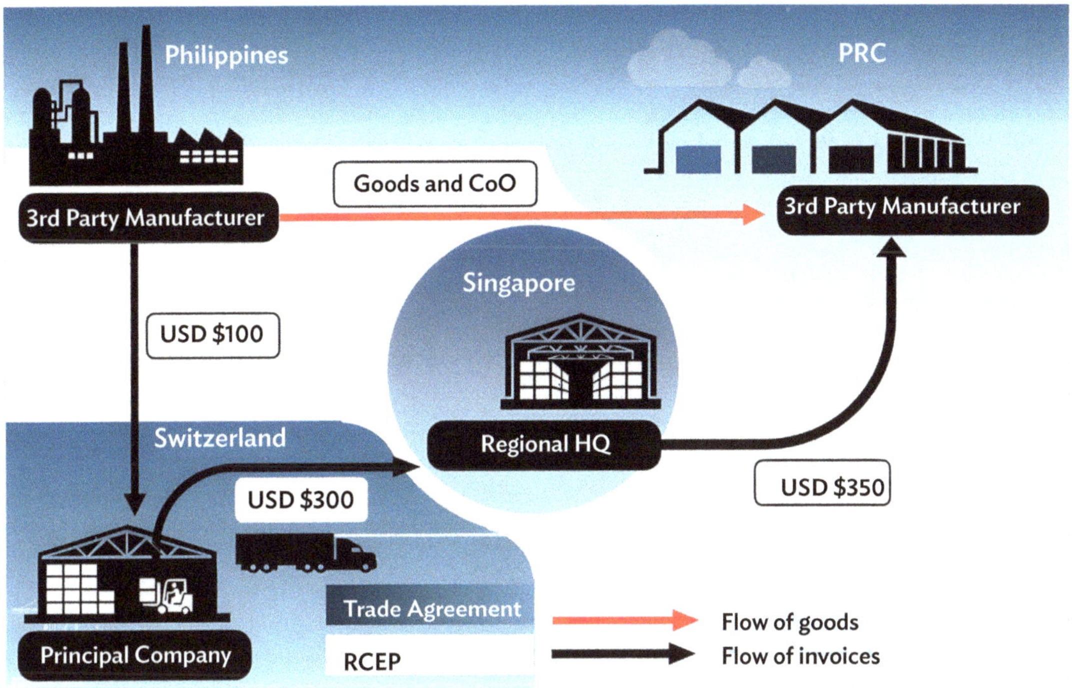

CoO = certificate of origin, HQ = headquarters,PRC = People's Republic of China, RCEP = Regional Comprehensive Economic Partnership.
Source: Elaboration from Anliker (2023).

Article 3.20 of the RCEP foresees that in such situations, no authority should deny the preferential origin of the goods:

"An importing Party shall not deny a claim for preferential tariff treatment for the sole reason that an invoice was not issued by the exporter or producer of a good provided that the good meets the requirements in this Chapter" (Article 3.20: Third-Party Invoicing of the RCEP).

However, these mismatches have caused many importing countries and customs authorities to deny preferential importation of such goods. In some countries, bilateral discussions with the authority were required to allow preferential importation. Some authorities interpreted the word "third" literally and did not allow preferential importation if more than three parties were involved in the entire transaction (Figure 5).[32]

Third-country or third-party invoicing procedure allows originating goods exported to an FTA member country with a preferential CO to qualify for preferential tariff treatment even if the accompanying sales invoice is issued by:

(a) a company located in a non-FTA member country (third-country invoicing); or

(b) an exporter in an FTA member country for the account of the company (third-party invoicing).

[32] See Anliker (2023). https://hdl.handle.net/1814/76084.

In a number of cases, the wording of third-country invoicing has been interpreted as if the invoice had to be necessarily issued in a third country rather than in a member of the FTA. This misunderstanding is confirmed by the fact that the issue of third-country invoicing often arose in the context of the SCAROO (Table 3). There was also a requirement that the words "SUBJECT OF THIRD PARTY/ COUNTRY INVOICE" and the name of the company issuing the third-party invoicing should be indicated on the CO. This requirement created major practical difficulty for the exporters. While an exporter was able to indicate the name of the first company issuing the third-party invoicing, it was almost impossible for the exporter to identify the second or the third companies involved in issuing invoices. Hence, the exporter could not indicate on the certificate the name of the final third party. This resulted in importing FTA parties denying preferential access.

A CO accompanied by a third-country invoice will only be approved if the exporter of the goods indicates "third-country invoicing" in the certificate, along with information such as the name and country of the company issuing the invoice.

Table 8 sets out the third-party invoicing provisions in each ASEAN+1 FTA, RCEP, and CPTPP.

Table 8: Third-Country and Third-Party Invoicing Provisions in ASEAN+1 FTAs, RCEP, and CPTPP

ASEAN FTA	Rule/Article	Third-Country Invoicing
ATIGA	Annex 8, Rule 23	1. *Relevant Government authorities in the importing Member State shall accept Certificates of Origin (Form D) in cases where the sales invoice is issued either by a company located in a third country or by an ASEAN exporter for the account of the said company, provided that the goods meet the requirements of Chapter 3 of this Agreement.* 2. *The exporter shall indicate "third-country invoicing" and such information as name and country of the company issuing the invoice in the Certificate of Origin (Form D).*
AANZFTA	Annex on OCPs to Chapter 3 (rules of origin) as amended by the First Protocol, Rule 22	THIRD-COUNTRY INVOICING Rule 13 1. An importing Party shall not deny a claim for preferential tariff treatment for the sole reason that the sales invoice was issued by a company located in a third country other than the AANZFTA exporting or importing country, provided that the good meets the requirements in Chapter 3 (Rules of Origin). 2. The words "SUBJECT OF THIRD COUNTRY INVOICE (name of the first company issuing the third-country invoice)" shall appear on the Certificate of Origin.[a]
AIFTA	Annex 2, Appendix D, Article 22	*The Customs Authority in the importing Party shall accept an AIFTA Certificate of Origin where the sales invoice is issued either by a company located in a third country or an AIFTA exporter for the account of the said company, provided that the product meets the requirements of the AIFTA Rules of Origin.*

continued on the next page

Table 8 continued.

ASEAN FTA	Rule/Article	Third-Country Invoicing
ACFTA	Amending Protocol, Annex 1, Attachment A, Rule 23	*The Customs Authority of the importing Party shall accept a CO (Form E) in cases where the sales invoice is issued either by a company located in a third country or by an ACFTA exporter for the account of the said company, provided that the product meets the requirements of the Rules of Origin for the ACFTA. The invoice-issuing third party can be an ACFTA Party or non-ACFTA Party. The original invoice number or the third-party invoice number shall be indicated in Box 10 of the CO (Form E), the exporter and consignee must be located in the Parties and the third-party invoice shall be attached to the CO (Form E) when presenting the said CO (Form E) to the Customs Authority of the importing Party.*
AJCEP	Annex 4, Rule 3(1)	*For the purposes of claiming preferential tariff treatment, the following shall be submitted to the customs authority of the importing Party by the importer:* (a) a valid CO; and (b) other documents as required in accordance with the laws and regulations of the importing Party (e.g., invoices, including third-country invoices, and a through bill of lading issued in the exporting Party).
AKFTA	Annex 3, Appendix 1, Rule 21	1. *Customs authority in the importing Party may accept COsin cases where the sales invoice is issued either by a company located in a third country or by an exporter for the account of the said company, provided that the good meets the requirements of Annex 3.* 2. *The exporter of the goods shall indicate "third-country invoicing" and such information as name and country of the company issuing the invoice in the CO.*
RCEP	Article 3.20	An importing Party shall not deny a claim for preferential tariff treatment for the sole reason that an invoice was not issued by the exporter or producer of a good provided that the good meets the requirements in this Chapter.
CPTPP	Paragraph 4 of article 3.18	A Party shall not reject a claim for preferential tariff treatment for the sole reason that the invoice was issued in a non-Party. If an invoice is issued in a non-Party, a Party shall require that the certification of origin be separate from the invoice.

AANZFTA = ASEAN-Australia-New Zealand Free Trade Area, ACFTA = ASEAN-China Free Trade Area, AIFTA = ASEAN-India Free Trade Area , AJCEP = ASEAN-Japan Comprehensive Economic Partnership, AKFTA = ASEAN-Korea Free Trade, ASEAN = Association of Southeast Asian Nations, ATIGA = ASEAN Trade in Goods Agreement, CPTPP = Comprehensive and Progressive Agreement for Trans-Pacific Partnership, CO = certificate of origin, FTA = free trade agreement, OCP = operational certification procedures, RCEP = Regional Comprehensive Economic Partnership.

[a] As last amended in the second protocol of AANZA available at https://www.dfat.gov.au/trade/agreements/in-force/aanzfta/official-documents/second-protocol-to-amend-the-agreement-establishing-asean-australia-new-zealand-free-trade-area-aanzfta.

Sources: Aforementioned free trade agreements.

The comparative reading of the provisions related to third-country invoicing shows wide disparities on the treatment of this OCP among ASEAN+1 FTAs, RCEP, and CPTPP. While the wording of the third-country provision is somewhat similar in ATIGA and ASEAN+ 1 FTAs, a different formulation is used in RCEP and CPTPP by prescribing that a claim for preferential tariff treatment should not be denied for sole reason that the invoice was not issued by the exporter or producer. There are, however, significant differences between RCEP and CPTPP in the formulation's wording.

The picture concerning the use of third-country invoicing is better completed by adding the specific requirements that have to be filled in on COs (Table 9).

Table 9: Comparison of Third-Country Invoicing Provisions in ASEAN+1 FTAs, RCEP, and CPTPP

ATIGA	AJCEP	AIFTA	ACFTA	AANZFTA	AKFTA	RCEP (Box 17)
THIRD-COUNTRY INVOICING: In cases where invoices are issued by a third country, "the Third Country Invoicing" box should be ticked (√)	THIRD-COUNTRY INVOICING: In cases where invoices are issued by a third country, in accordance with Rule 3 (d) of Implementing Regulations, the "Third Country Invoicing" box in box 13 should be ticked (√). In an exceptional case where the invoice issued in a third country is not available at the time of issuance of the certificate of origin, the invoice number and the date of the invoice issued by the exporter to whom the certificate of origin is issued should be indicated in box 10. The "Third Country Invoicing" in box 13 should be ticked, and it should be indicated in box 7 that the goods will be subject to another invoice to be issued in a third country for the importation into the importing Party.	THIRD-COUNTRY INVOICING: In cases where invoices are issued by a third country, "Third Country Invoicing" in Box 13 should be ticked (√)	THIRD-PARTY INVOICING: In cases where invoices are issued by a third country, "the Third-Party Invoicing" in Box 13 shall be ticked (√).	SUBJECT OF THIRD-PARTY INVOICE: In cases where invoices used for the importation are issued in a third country, in accordance with Rule 22 of the Operational Certification Procedures, the "SUBJECT OF THIRD-PARTY INVOICE" box in Box 13should be ticked (√)	THIRD-COUNTRY INVOICING: In cases where invoices are issued by a third country, "the Third Country Invoicing" box should be ticked (√) and such information as name and country of the company issuing the invoice shall be indicated in box 7.	INVOICES: Indicate the invoice number and date in Box 13. If multiple invoices are used, indicate the invoice number and date for each item. The invoice is the one issued for the importation of the good into the importing Party. In cases where invoices used for the importation are not issued by the exporter or producer, in accordance with Article 3.20 of Chapter 3 of the Agreement, the "Third-party invoicing" box in Box 17 should be ticked (√)

AANZFTA = ASEAN-Australia-New Zealand Free Trade Area, ACFTA = ASEAN–China Free Trade Area, AIFTA = ASEAN–India Free Trade Area , AJCEP = ASEAN–Japan Comprehensive Economic Partnership, AKFTA = ASEAN–Korea Free Trade, ASEAN = Association of Southeast Asian Nations, ATIGA = ASEAN Trade in Goods Agreement, CCPTP = Comprehensive and Progressive Agreement for Trans-Pacific Partnership, FTA = free trade agreement, RCEP = Regional Comprehensive Economic Partnership.
Source: Compiled by the authors based on FTAs' legal texts.

4.1.4 Small Consignments

The waiver of proof of origin for small consignments is one of the most obvious examples of trade facilitation. Yet, even in this area, ATIGA and ASEAN+1 FTAs have introduced a set of rather different and stringent requirements. First, ATIGA, ASEAN+1 FTAs, and RCEP waive the requirement of proof of origin only if the consignment from the exporting member state does not exceed the value of $200 free on board (FOB). In the case of ATIGA and ASEAN+1 FTAs, the exporter still has to sign a simplified declaration. Compared with the EU, in ASEAN FTAs the simplified declaration by the exporter is accepted up to a limit of €6,000. And in the case of Japan's GSP, it is up to ¥200,000, approximately $1,326 or €1,226 (as of 22 October 2024 forex rate).

The RCEP text appears quite convoluted as it limits the waiver to $200 FOB but does not refer to the need for a simplified exporter declaration. The CPTPP raises the limit to $1,000 FOB without mentioning the need for a simplified exporter declaration.

Table 10 indicates the relevant provisions on documentary requirements for each ASEAN+1 FTA, RCEP, and CPTPP.

Table 10: Comparison of Provisions on Waiver of Prooof of Origin for Small Consigments in ASEAN+1 FTAs, RCEP, and CPTPP

FTA	Waiver of Certificate of Origin Requirement (Legal Text)	Threshold
ATIGA	**Annex 8, Rule 15** In the case of consignments of goods originating in the exporting Member State and not exceeding $200 FOB, the production of a Proof of Origin shall be waived and the use of simplified declaration by the exporter that the goods in question have originated in the exporting Member State will be accepted. Goods sent through the post not exceeding $200 FOB shall also be similarly treated.	$200 FOB
AANZFTA	**Second Amending Protocol, Annex 3A, Rule 16** 3. Notwithstanding Paragraphs 1 and 2, the importing Party may not require a Proof of Origin for the purposes of claiming preferential tariff treatment if: (a) the customs value of the importation does not exceed $200 or the equivalent amount in the importing Party's currency or any higher amount as the importing Party may establish based on its laws, regulations or administrative practices; or (b) it is a good for which the importing Party has waived the requirement, provided that the importation does not form part of a series of importations carried out or planned for the purpose of evading compliance with the importing Party's laws and regulations governing claims for preferential tariff treatment under this Agreement.	$200

continued on the next page

Table 10 continued.

FTA	Waiver of Certificate of Origin Requirement (Legal Text)	Threshold
ACFTA	**Amending Protocol, Attachment A, Rule 16** (a) In the case of the consignment of products originating in the exporting Party and not exceeding $200 FOB, the production of a Certificate of Origin (Form E) shall be waived and the use of a simplified declaration by the exporter that the products in question originated in the exporting Party shall be accepted. Products sent through the post not exceeding $200 FOB shall also be similarly treated. (b) Waivers provided for in paragraph (a) shall not be applicable when it is established by the customs authorities of the importing Party that the importation forms part of a series of importations that may reasonably be considered to have been undertaken or arranged for the purpose of avoiding the submission of a Certificate of Origin or Certificates of Origin.	$200 FOB
AJCEP	**Annex 4, Rule 3** 2. A Certificate of Origin shall not be required for an importation of a consignment of originating goods of the exporting Party whose aggregate customs value does not exceed $200 or its equivalent amount in the Party's currency, or such higher amount as the importing Party may establish.	$200
AKFTA	**Rule 11 of Appendix 1 to Annex 3** A Certificate of Origin shall not be required for: (a) a good originating in the territory of a Party which does not exceed $200 FOB: or (b) a good sent by post from the territory of a Party which does not exceed $200 FOB, provided that the importation does not form part of one or more importations that may reasonably be considered to have been undertaken or arranged for the purpose of avoiding the submission of a Certificate of Origin.	$200 FOB
RCEP	Notwithstanding paragraphs 1 and 2, the importing Party may not require a Proof of Origin if: (a) the customs value of the importation does not exceed $200 or the equivalent amount in the importing Party's currency or any higher amount as the importing Party may establish; or (b) it is a good for which the importing Party has waived the requirement, provided that the importation does not form part of a series of importations carried out or planned for the purpose of evading compliance with the importing Party's laws and regulations governing claims for preferential tariff treatment under this Agreement.	$200
CPTPP	**Chapter 3, Article 3.23: Waiver of Certification of Origin** No Party shall require a certification of origin if: (a) the customs value of the importation does not exceed $1,000 or the equivalent amount in the importing Party's currency or any higher amount as the importing Party may establish; or (b) it is a good for which the importing Party has waived the requirement or does not require the importer to present a certification of origin, provided that the importation does not form part of a series of importations carried out or planned for the purpose of evading compliance with the importing Party's laws governing claims for preferential tariff treatment under this Agreement.	$1,000

AANZFTA = ASEAN-Australia-New Zealand Free Trade Area, ACFTA = ASEAN–China Free Trade Area, AJCEP = ASEAN–Japan Comprehensive Economic Partnership, AKFTA = ASEAN–Korea Free Trade, ASEAN = Association of Southeast Asian Nations, ATIGA = ASEAN Trade in Goods Agreement, CCPTP = Comprehensive and Progressive Agreement for Trans-Pacific Partnership, FTA = free trade agreement, RCEP = Regional Comprehensive Economic Partnership.
Source: Compiled by the authors based on the FTAs' legal texts.

4.2 Approved Exporters

Approved exporters have been a trade-facilitating opportunity introduced in the EU FTA progressively since the 1990s in FTAs entered with partner countries. Under the approved exporter method, an exporter may request to be granted the authority to issue an origin declaration—i.e., self-certification.

The exporter has to submit the request to the competent certifying authority and has to fulfill a series of requirements that the EU legislation summarizes has been reliable, not be subject to bankruptcy proceedings, or being in arrears of customs duties and taxes.

According to the EU guidelines,[33] the following elements should be submitted to the certifying authority to request approved exporter status:

- Data on the organization of the company
- Name of employee responsible for preferential transactions
- Accounting system for differentiating goods with or without preferential origin status (also information about IT system in use)
- Treatment of preferential documents (evidence of origin the applicant is going to hold)
    - Documents that must be detained by the applicant
    - Book-keeping system for guaranteeing that the applicant is in possession of all documents proving preferential origin
- Use of a customs procedure in the processing of the product, in particular authorization for inward processing, in order to avoid any incompatibility with a prohibition of duty drawback clause.
- Commitments of the exporter in case the authorization is issued:
    - to supply at all times evidence of the originating status of the exported goods,
    - to keep the evidence of the originating status 3 or more years (depending on the period mentioned in the preferential arrangement),
    - to make out an origin declaration only for products for which all evidence or accounting elements required to prove the preferential origin are held at the time of the export , and
    - when the possibility of not signing origin declarations (a signature waiver) is requested a written undertaking has to be submitted

The EU guidelines provide that a request for approved exporter status should be dealt within 120 days of the request and that the status of approved exporter may be granted either for an unlimited or limited time span. Where the EU and FTA partner countries use the approved exporter method, the implementation and the granting of approved exporter status is left with certifying authorities of the Parties. Hence, certifying authorities need to be provided with guidelines to reduce the room for discretionary practices within the EU.

The system of approved exporter has been used by ASEAN within ATIGA (as discussed in Section 6) and most recently in RCEP.

---

33 Available at https://taxation-customs.ec.europa.eu/system/files/2019-02/guidance-on-approved-exporters.pdf.

Box 4: Implementation of 'Approved Exporter' Status Under RCEP in the People's Republic of China

Order No. 254 of the General Administration of Customs[a] outlines the implementation of the approved exporter status by the People's Republic of China (PRC) under the Regional Comprehensive Economic Partnership. According to a recent summary by Deloitte:

"Qualifications of 'approved exporter'. An 'approved exporter' is a Chinese exporter approved by Chinese Customs to be eligible to issue declarations of origin which can be accepted as proof of origin under the relevant free trade agreements signed by the PRC.

To qualify as an approved exporter, the exporter must satisfy all of the following three conditions:

- *The exporter must understand the rules of origin under relevant preferential trade agreements so that it is able to correctly apply the rules to determine the originating status;*
- *The exporter must have a robust management system of documents supporting the originating status so that the management records can be traced and tracked in customs inspections; and*
- *The exporter must be recognized as an advanced customs certified enterprise (i.e., Chinese version of 'Authorized Economic Operator (AEO)').*

Application of 'approved exporter' status

To apply for 'approved exporter' status, an exporter must submit a written application to the in-charge customs authorities. Within 30 days of the application submission, the customs authorities should review the applicant's status, decide whether to grant the 'approved exporter' status, and notify the applicant of the decision in writing.

The 'approved exporter' status is valid for 3 years. Within a 3-month period prior to the status expiration, an approved exporter may apply for a renewal for another 3 years.

Chinese Customs has established a computerized system to manage approved exporters. All declarations of origin must be issued by an approved exporter through the system."

[a] General Administration of Customs of the People's Republic of China. 2021. Order No. 254: *Measures of the Customs of the People's Republic of China for the Administration of Approved Exporters.* November 23. https://www-lawinfochina-com.translate.goog/display.aspx?id=37026&lib=law&_x_tr_sch=http&_x_tr_sl=zh-CN&_x_tr_tl=en&_x_tr_hl=en&_x_tr_pto=sc.

Source: Deloitte. (2021), and Order No. 254 of the General Administration of Customs of 23 November 2021.

The approved exporter method introduced by the PRC in RCEP and other FTAs (presented in Box 4) is aligned with another initiative under the Duty-Free Quota Free initiative for least developed countries (LDCs), where the PRC government has introduced a system of self-certification for products/exporters that have previously been granted an approved advanced origin ruling.

One peculiarity of the PRC's approved exporter method is that the declaration of origin of the approved exporter must be issued through the computerized system set up by PRC customs. This appears to contradict the usual concept of approved exporter, which is typically understood to allow an exporter, once approved, to freely self-certify origin declarations.

4.3 Registered Exporter

The major concrete example of registered exporter stems from an EU initiative under the 2003 "*Green paper on the future of rules of origin in preferential trade agreements.*"[34] This publication reviews possible options to manage proof of origin and OCPs in various EU FTAs and preferential-trading arrangements. At that time the EU method of proof of origin and OCP were centered on certifying authorities and exchange of stamps, and, in the case of some FTAs, the existence of the approved exporters.

The need for a review of the EU method based on a certification authority was motivated by a series of internal cases at the European Court of Justice. This case law made the recovery of customs duties difficult when the importers could demonstrate their good faith by relying on a wrongly issued CO.[35]

The "green paper" and series of actions that followed marked the beginning of the journey of the EU toward a progressive but decisive move from an administration of COs based on the existence of certifying authorities, to an exporter-based system, known as Registered Exporter (REX).

Incremental implementation of the REX system started with the EU GSP. From 2017, exporters in EU GSP beneficiary countries had to self-register in the European Commission's newly established REX system. Beneficiary countries not yet ready to implement the system were given a series of transitional arrangements

The REX system is based on an IT system provided by the European Commission. Although the EU's intention was to limit the use of REX to the EU GSP, it is now increasingly used in many EU FTAs, including those with Japan, Singapore, and Viet Nam. The REX system provides the necessary flexibility to be used by EU FTA partners. For example, Zimbabwe is applying the REX system when exporting to the EU under its FTA with the EU. However, whereas Viet Nam has so far opted to maintain a CO-based system when exporting to the EU, the EU is adopting the REX system in the other direction of trade, from EU to Viet Nam.

To become a REX, any exporter, producer, or trader established in the EU[36] has to enter the REX website and provide a number of basic information contained in the application form: the exporter's name, address, and identification number; additional contact details (optional); whether the exporter is a trader, producer, or both; and an indicative list of goods that the exporter intends to export under the preferential trade agreements.

34 Available at http://aei.pitt.edu/37759/1/COM_(2003)_787_final.pdf.

35 See judgment of the Court of First Instance of the European Communities of 10 May 2001 in the "Turkish televisions" case (Joined cases T-186/97, Kaufring AG and Others)

36 Definition (31) of Article 5 of the UCC: "person established in the customs territory of the Union" means: (a) in the case of a natural person, any person who has their habitual residence in the customs territory of the Union; (b) in the case of a legal person or an association of persons, any person having its registered office, central headquarters or a permanent business establishment in the customs territory of the Union.

As contained in the guidelines of the EU Commission, the list of goods to be included in the registration pages is indicative, (either HS chapter numbers or heading numbers).[37] That an exporter might make a statement on origin for products not covered by this list is not a reason for refusal of the statement on origin. However, customs authorities in the importing party could consider this situation as needing verification (on the grounds of reasonable doubt).

Positive features of the REX system include:

- The procedure for applying to become a registered exporter is a one-off event. Once the exporter has been registered, it may use the registration number for all its exports under preferential arrangements where the system of certification of origin applied is the REX system, with no additional formality.
- The REX exporter's statement of origin is short, relatively simple, and can be made on commercial documents.[38] The statement of origin does not even need to be signed in certain FTAs.

Critical aspects include:

- The content of the "statement on origin" to be issued by the REX exporter is relatively simple but is not harmonized among all EU FTAs. Its content may vary, although not significantly so, depending on the FTA. This, in turn, means that the exporter has to be aware that a distinct statement of origin needs to be made depending on the country of destination.
- REX registration is possible only for firms established in the EU. making difficult for multinational companies established outside the EU to become a registered exporter (Trabucco 2023).

4.4 Self-Certification by Any Exporter/Importer

Self-certification by any exporter is a method where certifying authorities are not involved in the issuance of the proof of origin. The main difference from the other categories of self-certification by exporter is that the exporter does not need to register or be approved by the certifying authorities.

That noted, subcategories exist in the format of such self-certification (and where such certification has to be made or could be made). The different methods can be summarized as follows:

- **Any format of self-certification is acceptable as long as it contains the minimum data requirements and the prescribed statement.**[39] This is the case of the CPTPP where the content of the minimum data requirements are contained in Annex 3B of the CPTPP agreement.[40] There is no need to preregister. In short, there is no standard certificate template, but the declaration must include the statement given in part 9 of Annex 3B.[41]

[37] See https://taxationcustoms.ec.europa.eu/system/files/202205/Registered%20Exporter%20System%20%28REX%29%20-%20Guidance%20document.doc.pdf.

[38] There are a series of definitions for that could be considered "commercial documents." For instance, a bill of lading is not considered a commercial document as it is issued by a freight forwarder or a shipping company.

[39] There is a clear definition of what minimum requirement are in each FTA using such a method.

[40] As discussed in Section 9.2, the CPTPP permits some parties not to apply such a self-certification for as long as 12 years.

[41] The statement is as follows: "I certify that the goods described in this document qualify as originating and the information contained in this document is true and accurate. I assume responsibility for proving such representations and agree to maintain and present upon request or to make available during a verification visit, documentation necessary to support this certification."

- **The self-declaration has a specific wording**. This is the case of the EU–Canada Comprehensive Economic and Trade Agreement (CETA). A specific wording of the statement of origin is common to many FTAs. In the case of CETA such statement may be made by any exporter without preregistration.[42] The CETA rules do not require a formal certificate to obtain tariff benefits.

This method can be considered as one of the most liberal, given the absence of any preregistration mechanisms by certifying authorities. In addition, under the CPTPP, the amount of data and details requested appear to be legitimate and not overly demanding. The CETA method requires a specific format of statement to be made but, in reality, appears even easier to comply with given the simplicity of the text of the declaration.

[42] The statement is a follows: "(Period: from/to (1))The exporter of the products covered by this document (customs authorization No ... (2)) declares that, except where otherwise clearly indicated, these products are of ...(3) preferential origin. (4) (Place and date) (5) (Signature and printed name of the exporter)." A footnote 2 clarifies the following concerning EU exporters: "When the origin declaration is completed by an approved or registered exporter the exporter's customs authorization or registration number must be included. A customs authorization number is required only if the exporter is an approved exporter. When the origin declaration is not completed by an approved or registered exporter, the words in brackets must be omitted or the space left blank." For Canadian exporters: "The exporter's Business Number assigned by the Government of Canada must be included. Where the exporter has not been assigned a business number, the field may be left blank."

5. Electronic Certificates of Origin

The proliferation of electronic certificate of origin (e-CO) methods and solutions to the certification of origin has been steadily increasing in the last decade and continues to grow. There is an increasing number of IT solutions that are being elaborated and ambitions that are flagged as offering the fastest and best trade-facilitating solutions.

Faced by this continuous evolution, it is necessary to adopt a series of definitions to get better oriented in a new "science."

In a recent study,[43] the WCO provides a series of basic definitions such as:

1. Electronic Certificate of Origin (e-CO): refers to a CO where the application and issuance are completed electronically and normally signed and stamped digitally by government authority or body empowered to issue it.
2. Electronic Data Exchange for Certificates of Origin refers to the electronic exchange of COs or data relating to certification of origin between the relevant authorities.

These definitions are useful to distinguish steps reflecting two separate stages of what is generally considered an e-CO. Most methods today involve the issuance of an e-CO by the certifying authorities to an exporter who has applied for one online. Once the e-CO is issued, the exporter will forward it to the importer for submission to customs in the importing country. This is the situation described in point 1 above.

The exchange of electronic data for a COs depicts a further step: the issuing certifying authority electronically transmits the e-CO or data related to origin to the respective certifying authorities of the importing country for customs clearance. The ASEAN Single Window e-CO system currently being implemented could serve as an example of this further significant step.

In reality, this is more complicated and varied. While the full implementation of the ATIGA Form D was to be fully operational on 1 January 2024, some ASEAN member states are still reporting implementation challenges.

[43] WCO. 2024. *Study on the Digitalization of the Certificate of Origin*. https://www.wcoomd.org/-/media/wco/public/global/pdf/topics/origin/instruments-and-tools/origin-certification/study-on-the-digitalization-of-the-certificate-of-origin-en.pdf.

6. The Evolution of ATIGA Form D: From Self-Certification to ASEAN Single Window

As discussed in Section 4.1, the ASEAN intergovernmental machinery has continuously reported difficulties in implementing the various iteration of ASEAN rules of origin and OCPs. Such difficulties derived from a combination of incomplete or unclear drafting of the rules of origin legal texts and zealous processing of COs during export and import transactions. The processing of COs overemphasized the verification of paper documentation, rather than checking the substantive elements related to the origin of the goods and the underlying facts.

In other words, ASEAN certifying authorities devote much time and resources to check whether Form D, even in its new e-CO version, conforms with the ATIGA requirements rather to check whether the goods are originating. This explains previous ASEAN intergovernmental reports of low utilization rates as early as 2010 (Inama and Sim 2015). ASEAN member states have not consistently taken reports of low utilization into consideration. The finding of the 2010 report was simply noted and forwarded by SEOM to the AFTA Council. In 2021, an ASEAN secretariat study reiterated low average utilization rates of ATIGA of around 50% during 2016–2018 (Inama, Crivelli, and Ha 2022). This study was mandated by the 34th AFTA Council Meeting and the ASEAN Secretariat was asked to identify sectors with low ATIGA utilization using data provided by member states. The report and its findings of low utilization were discussed at relevant ASEAN meeting and member states were asked to provide information about which domestic regulations could contribute to low ATIGA utilization. Most responded that the main reason for low utilization was that similar preferential tariff rates under ATIGA and ASEAN+1 FTAs gave traders the flexibility to utilize other ASEAN+1 FTAs besides ATIGA.

Thus, rather than focusing on why ATIGA utilization rates were low and attempting to improve them by making PSROs and OCPs more attractive to businesses, ASEAN member states argued that other ASEAN+1 FTAs could provide better trading opportunities than ATIGA.

Difficulties with traditional methods of certification based on the exchange of signatures and stamps triggered the introduction of a self-certification initiative. The 22nd AFTA Council Meeting in August 2008 mandated improvements to the AFTA Rules of Origin and certification procedures in line with the ASEAN Economic Cooperation 2015 objectives. The ASEAN Self-Certification System introduced the concept of "certified exporters" to declare that their products have satisfied the 'ASEAN origin' criteria according to the model adopted by the EU of approved exporters (as discussed in Section 4.2). The introduction of certified exporters was expected to reduce compliance and administrative costs and minimize implementation issues (e.g., the rejection of the certificate of origin Form D).

The Self-Certification Pilot Project 1 (SCPP 1) was initiated in November 2010 by Brunei Darussalam, Malaysia, and Singapore. Thailand joined in October 2011. Initially, the process was reported as a success. The number of transactions covered by the program had increased during its first year of operation, and both participating companies and governments reported satisfaction with the program (USAID 2016).

However, some ASEAN member states expressed extreme skepticism about self-certification. Indonesia was reported as participating in the pilot program only if participating companies were limited to manufacturers, and if the authorized signatories per company were limited to three persons.

SCPP 1 was expected to run for 1 year, but the AFTA Council extended it up to 31 October 2012 allowing other ASEAN member states to initiate their own test run under a different set of conditions and rules.[44] Thus Indonesia, the Lao PDR, and the Philippines developed the Second Self-Certification Pilot Project (SCPP 2) implemented from 1 January 2014.

A USAID assessment in the Philippines reported in 2016 that, with 87 certified exporters in ASEAN under SCPP 2 and 388 under SCPP 1, it was clear that SCPP 1 was a more successful pilot (USAID 2016). However, some ASEAN member states regarded SCPP 1 as too liberal since it allowed trading companies to self-certificate. Their main concern remains the same today that the trading company does not manufacture the goods nor has direct access to underlying cost data (for RVC) and manufacturing information (for CTC) to confirm that the goods qualify as ASEAN-origin.

The SCPP 2 introduced a series of limitations compared to SCPP 1 specifying that: (i) self-certification should be limited to manufacturers/producers (excluding traders), (ii) the exchange of information should include a list of products that a certified exporter is authorized to self-certify with confirmation from the certification body that these products meet the ATIGA rules of origin, (iii) signatories to the invoice declaration should be limited to three per certified exporter and their specimen signatures must be circulated among the other ASEAN member states in the pilot project, (iv) an invoice declaration should strictly be made out on a commercial invoice, and (v) third-country invoicing will not be covered by the pilot project.

These restrictions explain why SCPP 2 was not as widely used as SCPP 1.

The *ASEAN-wide Self-Certification (AWSC) Guidebook* of 2020 reported that by September 2020, 505 companies were registered as certified exporters under SCPP 1. Both SCPP 1 and SCPP 2 were terminated in 2020 when the new Annex 8 of ATIGA OCP came into force, introducing the AWSC.[45]

The recent version of ATIGA Annex 8 (hereinafter referred to as the Annex) is a compromise among member states that sets out an ASEAN-wide form of certified exporter.[46] The Annex contains provisions for the progressive implementation of the certified exporters, including traders, and the establishment of the ASEAN-wide Self-Certification database, under the custody of the ASEAN Secretariat and accessible online by member states.

The status of certified exporters is subject to several requirements listed in Article 12A of the Annex. A trader can be a certified exporter on the condition that the trader: *"must have a "manufacturer's declaration" indicating the origin of the product to be subject to self-certification and readiness of the manufacturer to cooperate in retroactive check and verification visit should the need arise; and the exporter*

[44] 25th AFTA Council Meeting held in August 2011 in Manado, Indonesia.

[45] ANNEX 8, OPERATIONAL CERTIFICATION PROCEDURE FOR THE RULES OF ORIGIN UNDER CHAPTER 3, Endorsed at the 35th AFTA Council Meeting, 8 September 2021.

[46] Endorsed at the 35th AFTA Council Meeting of September 2021.

must have a sound bookkeeping and record keeping system, in accordance with the laws and regulations of the exporting Member State."[47]

In reality, the Annex both established and acknowledged the overlapping methods of proof of origin that exist in ATIGA.

The overlapping and coexistence of different methods of proof of origin are illustrated in Rule 2 of the Annex, which provides for the exchange of specimen signatures and official seals of the issuing authority, corresponding to the continuation of the use of the paper-based Form D alongside with the newly established ASEAN-wide Self-Certification database.

According to the coexistence of different methods of proof of origin, Rule 13 of the Annex provides that the importer may submit for customs clearance either:

(a) a CO (Form D) including supporting documents; or

(b) an origin declaration made out by a certified exporter, including supporting documents.

In addition to these proof of origin methods, the Annex introduces and codifies a rather revolutionary concept, although in a subdued manner, with Rule 26 establishing an equivalence among paper-based D and e-Form D marking an important milestone.

"Rule 26 Equivalence of Paper and Electronic Certificate of Origin (e-Form D)

1. *A Certificate of Origin (Form D) in electronic format may be applied for, issued, and accepted in lieu of one in paper format, with equivalent legal effect.*
2. *Rules 27 to 31 shall apply to Electronic Certificates of Origin (e-Form D). Unless otherwise specified in Rules 27 to 31, Rules 1 to 6, 8, 10, 11, 14 to 16, and 18 to 25 shall also apply to the processing of Electronic Certificates of Origin (e-Form D)."*

The Annex also refers to another important instrument of ASEAN regional integration: the Protocol on the Legal Framework (PLF) to implement the ASEAN Single Window.

In practice, even if not fully fledged in the Annex, the combination of the PLF and the Annex made it possible to establish the exchange of E-Form D via the ASEAN Single Window. This has initially been operational in Indonesia, Malaysia, Singapore, and Viet Nam.

As a side effect of the progressive implementation of e-Form D through the ASEAN Single Window, practitioners and stakeholders report a decline in use of both the certified exporter method and the ASEAN-wide Self-Certification database. ASEAN member states appear to be questioning the safety of the password to accede to the database, which is under the custody of the ASEAN Secretariat. Also, there is an increased tendency in ASEAN and in Asia more widely to invest in IT solutions through Electronic Origin Data Exchange Systems (EODES).

Several member states have developed EODES with a number of ASEAN+1 partners under bilateral memorandums of understanding. Indonesia, for example, has developed its national single window to accommodate EODES under:

[47] See paragraphs (f) and (g) of Rule 12 A of the Annex.

- Electronic Form AK (ASEAN–Korea FTA): Implemented in February 2020.
- Electronic Form E (ASEAN–China FTA): Implemented in October 2020.
- Electronic Form IJEPA (Indonesian–Japan Economic Partnership agreement): Implemented in June 2023.
- Electronic Form IKCEPA (Indonesia–Korea Comprehensive Economic Partnership Agreement): Implemented in February 2024.

An informal working group[48] of the WCO's Technical Committee on Rules of Origin presented a feasibility study on an Interconnectivity Framework for the Certificate of Origin at a February 2024 meeting.

As outlined in the study, the Interconnectivity Framework for Certificates of Origin aims to provide WCO partners negotiating bilateral or multilateral trade agreements on cross-border data exchange with a model for completing the technical annex for the exchange of COs. The declared objective of the framework is to develop interconnectivity systems in a cost-effective and efficient manner, allowing parties involved in multiple FTAs to use a compatible system for origin certification.

The study assesses the scope of interconnectivity and types of proof of origin, along with business process models and the data set needed to obtain an e-CO. Supplementary information on other methods for dealing with proof of origin, such as importer-based or self-certification, is included in the study's annexes.

While welcoming the study, concerns have been expressed at the Technical Committee on Rules of Origin over the possible implications and difficulties in implementing IT digital systems contained in the study. These digital systems require extensive expertise, capacity building, and resources for developing and changing legislation that are not commonly available in developing economies, especially LDCs. Difficulty with implementing e-Form D through the ASEAN Single Window in some ASEAN member states[49] requires caution, further study, and careful assessment. In addition, the current digitalization trend does not fully explore the option of self-certification used in many other countries in Asia and the Pacific, as well as in other regions. Better understanding and quantifying the pros and cons of the e-COsand self-certification would add value to the ongoing debate on possible models of proof of origin and OCPs. Ultimately, self-certification could also be subject to digitalization.

One inherent cross cutting limitation of EODES systems in Asia and the Pacific identified in this study is that they only or mainly cover the electronic exchange of an e-CO. However, customs clearance under FTAs requires further documentation, such as commercial invoices and documentary evidence of direct consignment. Field research and interviews with entities using EODES systems have found that current EODES systems do not provide for full interconnectivity of documents that are essential for preferential customs clearance.

48 See the WCO document "Feasibility Study on Interconnectivity Framework for Certificate of Origin based on Globally Networked Customs (GNC) Methodologies." Annex to Doc. OC0254Ea(OC/42/Feb. 2024). https://www.wcoomd.org/-/media/wco/public/global/pdf/topics/facilitation/ressources/permanent-technical-committee/243-244/pc0749eae1.pdf

49 See, for instance, the 2021 ASEAN Secretariat study utilization rates, where Malaysia reported "occasional technical issues under the ASW platform such as missing data elements and failure to send e-Form D delivery responses as well as technical issues due to different NSW platform might have lowered the trader's confidence in utilizing e-Form D."

Closer examination of literature on the operationalization of the ASEAN Single Window indicates that some advanced customs administrations are taking steps to include such key additional aspects of proof of origin and OCPs (such as third-country invoicing and back-to-back certificates of origin) in the current EODES system.[50]

Even as some administrations make progress, most EODES currently do not provide for the electronic transmission of key additional customs clearance documents. This observation invites further reflection on the comparative advantage of EODES over other methods of proof of origin, especially self-certification.

50 See, for instance, Submitting and Retrieving a Form D via the ASEAN Single Window (ASW) in International Connectivity Service (ICS) Last Revised: Apr 2023, Singapore Customs and Circular No: 19/202329 Concerning Updated Procedures involving the Electronic Origin Data Exchange System (EODES) between Singapore and China, September 2023, and the Application of for certificate of non-manipulation; and https://www.customs.gov.sg/files/businesses/ttsb-roo/Submitting_and_Retrieving_a_Form_D_via_the_ASEAN_Single_Window__ICS____updated_on_20_Mar_2024.pdf.

7. Lessons Learned from Free Trade Agreements with the European Union and the United States

While the Asia and Pacific region remains focused on finding the best method of proof of origin and OCPs, the EU and the US, together with countries in the region—mostly Australia and New Zealand, and to a certain extent Japan—are moving toward self-certification.

The EU operates a dual certification regime in most FTAs it has recently concluded: a conventional certification system based on certifying authorities and approved exporter in older FTAs on one hand and, on the other, a more modern self-certification scheme, REX (Sections 4.2 and 4.3).

Self-certification under REX or approved exporters consists of making out a declaration of a given model on the invoice ('invoice declaration') and is generally available to precleared exporters who have satisfied the authorities in the country of export that their documentation is reliable, or to exporters whose shipments are worth less than €6,000. In the case of REX, self-certification is available to any exporter who has registered with the REX database. Importantly, the EU has adopted the REX method in its recent FTAs, such as those with Japan and with ASEAN countries, and aims to expand its use during the renegotiations of some African FTAs.[51]

Self-certification is the only option under the United States, Mexico, and Canada Agreement, and in other US FTAs. Any exporter in US FTA partners can complete and sign a CO and send it to the importer. Yet, the US importer bears ultimate responsibility for the origin declaration by self-declaring the origin of the goods on the basis of their knowledge and the information provided by the exporter in a CO. The CPTPP text adopts the importer-based declaration, as discussed in Section 3. And as explained in section 4.1, even if the provision is accompanied by long transitional periods as specified in Annex 3A of Protocol 3 on rules of origin and procedures of the CPTPP, the final objective remains self-certification. The recent AANZFTA contains a provision to consider the adoption of an importer-based declaration during the review of OCPs. Finally, a footnote to paragraph 4 of Rule 3.10 on proof of origin of RCEP provides that Japan may adopt an importer-based system from the entry into force of RCEP.[52]

The insertion of such provisions for the adoption of an importer-based system, even in a distant future, indicates that many countries in Asia and the Pacific still envisage this method of self-certification as one of the best long-term objective.

[51] The agreement between the EU and Canada (CETA), EU–Japan FTA, EU–Viet Nam, EU–Singapore FTAs from 1 January 2023, the EU-UK FTA (EU-UK TCA), EU-Ghana FTA, and EU–Cote d Ivoire Economic Partnership Agreement, and EU–Eastern and Southern Africa Economic Partnership Agreement (ESA).

[52] Footnote 5 to paragraph 4 of Rule 3.16 of RCEP provides as follows: "Notwithstanding this paragraph, Japan may, from the date of the entry into force of this Agreement for it, consider a Declaration of Origin by an importer as a Proof of Origin in the same manner as Proof of Origin under paragraph 1. In that case, Japan shall not conduct a verification process by means referred to in subparagraphs 1(b) through (d) of Article 3.24 (Verification) regarding the Declaration of Origin by the importer. The Declaration of Origin shall only be completed by the importer where that importer has sufficient information to prove that the good qualifies as an originating good."

8. Survey of Firms in Viet Nam on Best Method of Proof of Origin

This section reports the main results of a survey carried out using a combination of questionnaires administered by directly contacting firms, sampling 20 firms for in-person interviews and verifications of results of an overall 222 firms carried out between 2023 and 2024.

Viet Nam has been selected as test ground since it has entered numerous overlapping FTAs and its firms have been exposed to a variety of methods of proof of origin. The survey's objective was to find out what firms considered best and most business-friendly practices for proof of origin and OPCs, with the results shown in Figure 6. The questions were tailored to the existing different methods of proof of origin in Viet Nam.

Of the respondents, 46.4% viewed e-COs via the ASEAN Single Window as the easiest system and the most business-friendly, followed by e-CO in PDF format (24.7%) and registered exporters (12.6%). Notably, 6.3% of the respondents found the traditional hard-copy certificate of origin issued by certifying authorities to be the easiest and most business-friendly option. While these findings may somewhat contrast with other evidence from this study, they should be interpreted within the specific context and mindset of firms in Viet Nam, as further explained below.

In-person detailed interviews with selected firms revealed that lack of knowledge and confidence in certifying compliance with rules of origin requirements was the primary reason the traditional method found support. Firms that are unsure or not educated about rules of origin prefer to rely on a certifying authority for the issuance of COs as, under this method, they receive guidance and support from the certifying authority.

Many firms responded that while self-certification of origin is convenient, they are concerned about potential problems, such as submitting incomplete or inaccurate documents.

As Figure 7 shows, the traditional method of hard-copy certificate of origin stamped by a certifying authority is not as convenient as an e-CO issued by ASEAN Single Window or an e-CO that is in PDF format. Firms consider the ASEAN Single Window or the e-CO as PDF to be more trade-facilitating when certifying authorities are involved in management of COs. This tallies with the study findings.

Figure 8 reports the views firms provided about the degree of easiness of origin certification procedures.

The right part of Figure 8 dealing with self-certification (starting from registered exporter through to declaration by the importer - see red dashed line) shows a large number of firms declaring that they had no awareness of the possibilities of self-certification (gray bar). In-person interviews and discussions with the certifying authority and the Viet Nam Chamber of Commerce shed light on this issue. Firms were either unaware of the opportunities available for approved exporters under ASEAN or the EU FTAs, or are discouraged from applying due to the complexity of the process and a lack of confidence.

Figure 7: The Easiest and Business-Friendly System

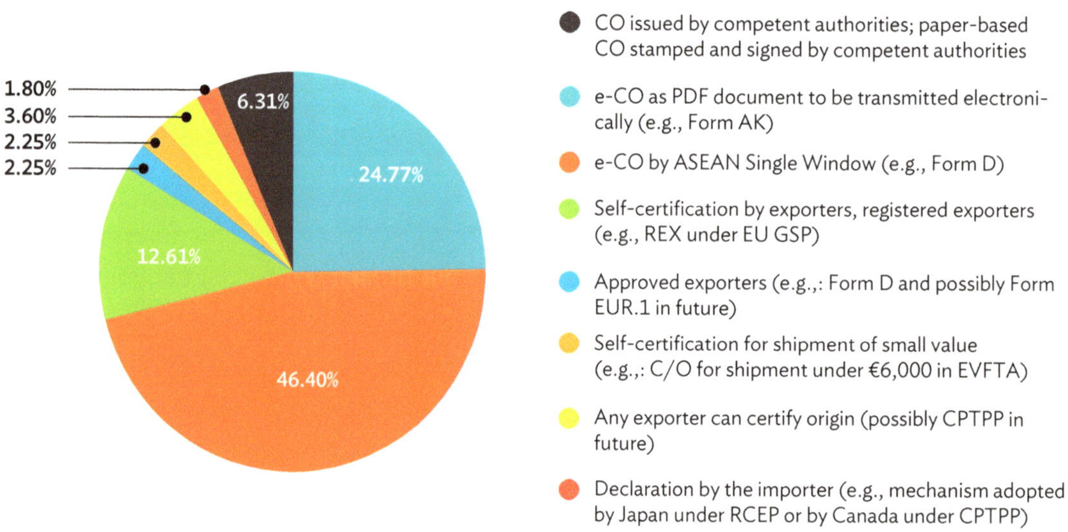

ASEAN = Association of Southeast Asian Nations, CO = certificate of origin, CPTPP = Comprehensive and Progressive Agreement for Trans-Pacific Partnership, e-CO = electronic certificate of origin, EU GSP = European Union Generalized System of Preferences, EVFTA = European Union-Vietnam Free Trade Agreement,
Source: 2023/2024 survey of firms in Viet Nam.

Figure 8: Degree of Easiness of Certification Procedures

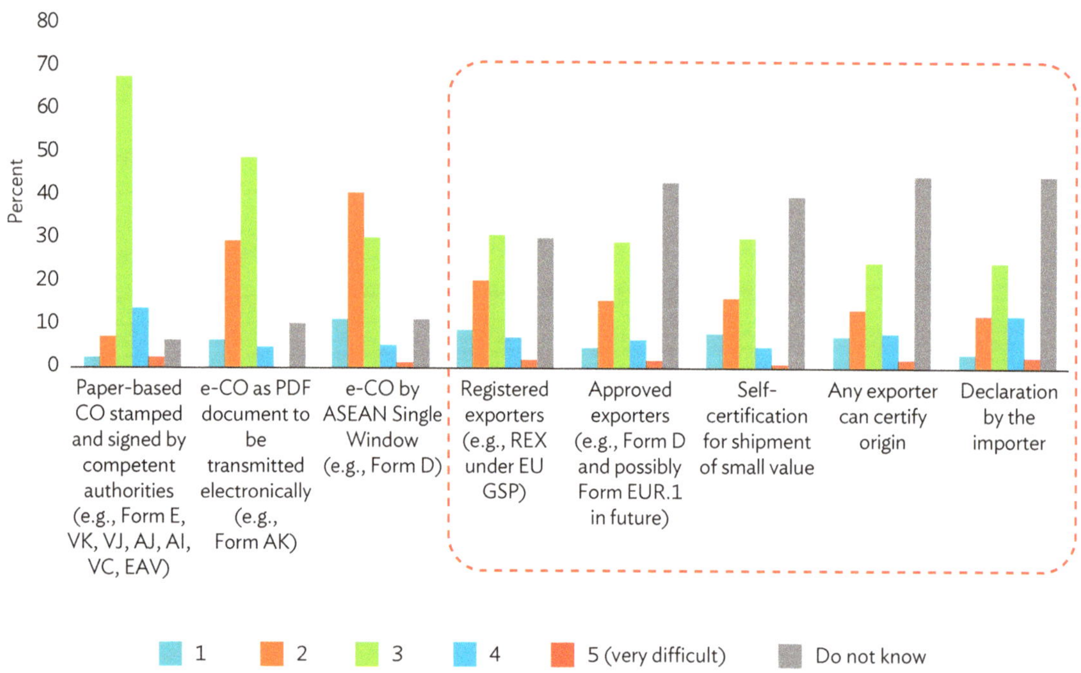

ASEAN = Association of Southeast Asian Nations, CO = certificate of origin, e-CO = electronic certificate of origin, EU GSP = European Union Generalized System of Preferences.
Source: 2023/2024 survey of firms in Viet Nam.

Additionally, they are equally uninformed about the possibility of self-certification under other FTAs or for small-value shipments. This finding aligns with the established approach of ASEAN member states toward OCPs. Some have demonstrated reservations about adopting self-certification and instead prefer to maintain a strong role for certifying authorities in managing compliance with rules of origin. These reservations have resulted in deeply rooted practices across ASEAN, including in Viet Nam, as reflected in the survey results.

Figure 9 completes the main findings of the survey and contributes to better understanding of the framework of the replies by firms who were requested to state to what extent they agreed with specific statements.

Figure 9: Survey Responses on Key Trade Facilitation Measures—Firms' Agreement with Statements on Compliance Cost Reduction and Certification Procedures

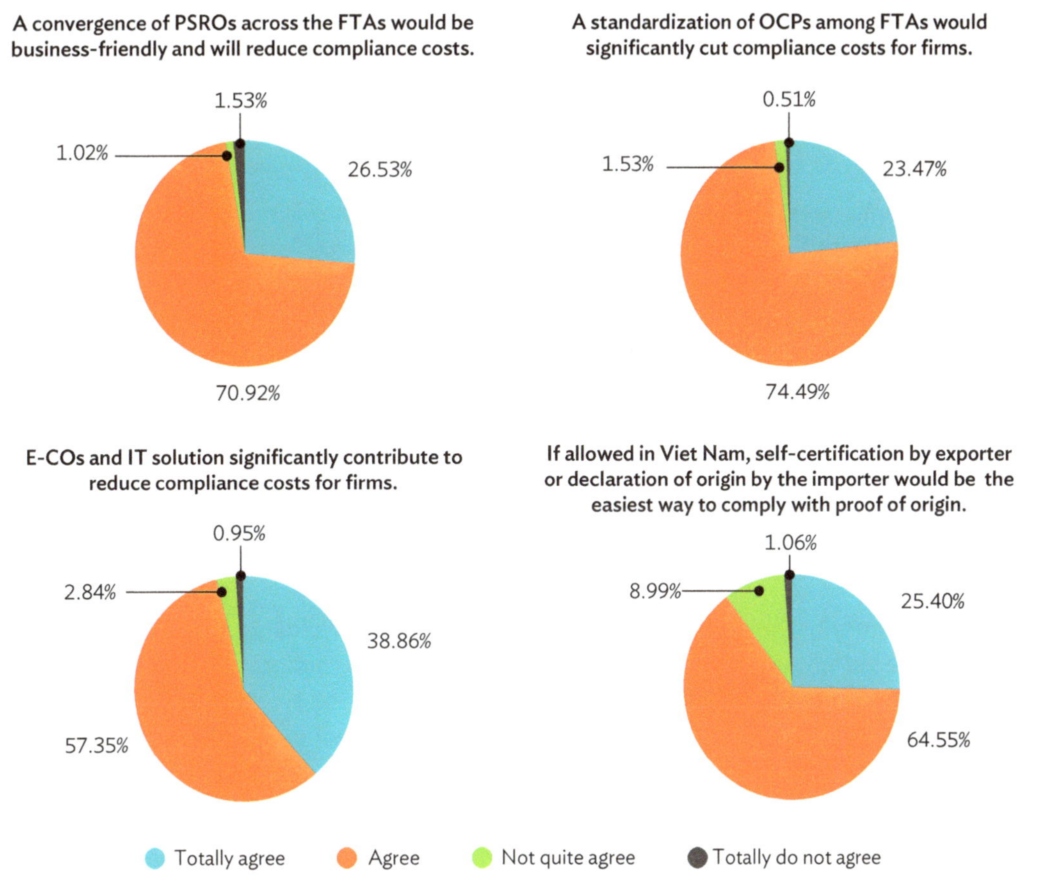

E-CO = electronic certificate of origin, FTA = free trade agreement, OCP = operational certification procedures, PSRO = product-specific rules of origin.
Source: 2023/2024 survey of firms in Viet Nam.

A large number of firms either totally agreed (27%) or agreed (71%) that convergence of product-specific rules of origin (PSRO) across FTAs would reduce compliance costs. The same holds true for a standardization or convergence of OCPs among FTAs, where 74% agree and 23% totally agree—bringing the total to 97%. These findings corroborate the case for convergence for both PSRO and OPCs. In the same vein, 39% of firms totally agreed and 57% agreed with the statement that IT solutions would significantly reduce compliance costs.

It is important to read such results in a country-specific context, as this may further explain circumstances influencing the questionnaire results and provide a better understanding the overall findings.

The results reflect the strong role of the Ministry of Industry and Trade serving as the certifying authority responsible for managing e-COs, whether through the ASEAN Single Window or other electronic formats. This prominent governmental role in overseeing proof of origin and OCPs appears to influence firms' behavior. While companies demonstrate a willingness to comply with rules of origin, they remain hesitant to take an active role in managing proof of origin due to the lack of incentives for self-certification. In this context, the responses by firms indicate that:

- In the case of proof of origin managed by a certifying authority, they prefer the ASEAN Single Window e-CO, where the certifying authority's role is less intrusive and time-consuming.
- When firms have the choice between methods of proof of origin administered by a certifying authority or self-certification, they opt for self-certification.

90% of the respondents indicated that self-certification would be the easiest way to comply with origin requirements if made available to them (Figure 9, lower right panel). This result highlights that the lack of knowledge about alternative proof of origin methods beyond those managed by the certifying authority aligns with the government's reservations about allowing self-certification. These reservations are reflected in the dual system in the EU–Viet Nam FTA, where Viet Nam has not stepped toward implementation of the REX system, even though it was already in use under the EU GSP until 1 January 2023. In addition, among RCEP and CPTPP options for the implementation of OCPs, Viet Nam has systematically taken advantage of any provisions to postpone the self-certification.

Although Viet Nam's Ministry of Industry and Trade reported to be providing extensive capacity-building activities, a large percentage of firms still admit to being unaware of some critical aspects of OCPs and self-certification methods. This lack of knowledge, coupled with the government's prominent role as the certifying authority, may act as a hurdle to the adoption of more trade-facilitating OCP practices, such as self-certification, and to the utilization of Viet Nam's FTAs.

Table 11: Utilization Rates of Viet Nam FTA, 2020–2022

FTA	CO Form	Rate of FTA Utilization (FTA certificate of origin value/total export value) (%) 2020	2021	2022
ATIGA	Form D	38.8	40.0	39.2
ACFTA	Form E	31.7	33.9	29.3
AKFTA	Form AK	52.1	50.9	50.9
VKFTA	Form VK			
AANZFTA	Form AANZ	40.2	39.2	39.3
AJCEP	Form AJ	37.9	34.7	34.7
VJEPA	Form VJ			
VCFTA	Form VC	65.5	61,8	64.6
AIFTA	Form AI	70.0	68.7	66.9
VN-EAEU FTA	Form EAV	29.6	39.0	59.4
Lao PDR	Form S	11.4	10.3	6.3
Cambodia	Form X	0.0	0.0	0.0
AHKFTA	Form AHK	0.05	0.1	0.14
CPTPP	Form CPTPP	4.0	6.3	4.9
VN-Cuba	Form VN-CU	0.5	–	–
EVFTA	Form EUR.1	14.8	20.2	25.9
UKVFTA	Form EUR.1 UK		17.2	23.5
RCEP	Form RCEP			0.67
Total		**33.1**	**32.7**	**33.6**

AANZFTA = ASEAN-Australia-New Zealand Free Trade Area, ACFTA = ASEAN–China Free Trade Area, AHKFTA = ASEAN–Hong Kong, China Free Trade Agreement, AIFTA = ASEAN–India Free Trade Area, AJCEP = ASEAN–Japan Comprehensive Economic Partnership, AKFTA = ASEAN–Korea Free Trade, ATIGA = ASEAN Trade in Goods Agreement, CO = certificate of origin, CPTPP = Comprehensive and Progressive Agreement for Trans-Pacific Partnership, EVFTA = EU-Vietnam Free Trade Agreement, FTA = free trade agreement, Lao PDR = Lao People's Democratic Republic, RCEP = Regional Comprehensive Economic Partnership, UKVFTA = UK-Vietnam Free Trade Agreement, VCFTA = Vietnam-Chile Free Trade Agreement, VJEPA = Vietnam-Japan Economic Partnership Agreement, VKFTA = Vietnam-Korea Free Trade Agreement, VN-Cuba = Vietnam-Cuba, VN-EAEU FTA = Vietnam-Eurasian Economic Union Free Trade Agreement.
Source: Viet Nam Ministry of Industry and Trade.

Table 11 reports persistently low utilization rates for all Viet Nam's FTAs, further underscoring the impact of these challenges. In addition, a 42% utilization rate in the EU for 2022, using a WTO-agreed method of calculation,[53] compares with 26% recorded by Viet Nam that year. Such a discrepancy may derive from the Ministry of Industry and Trade's inclusion of trade volumes with most-favored nation zero rates (duty free) in the calculation of utilization rates. While this approach differs from the WTO method commonly used for calculating utilization rates worldwide, it does not affect the overall observation that utilization rates are particularly low in most of Viet Nam's FTAs. In addition, EU data reported in Table 12 shows that transition from EU GSP to EU–Viet Nam FTA is slow. Overall, the low utilization rates of Viet Nam's FTAs seem to reflect the difficulties firms face in navigating the complexities of rules of origin, as highlighted in the survey results, signaling the need for reforms in OCP management .

[53] See WTO G/RO/M/68 of 2017: "After consultations, members had adopted the methodology proposed by the secretariat (paragraph 3.2 (a) of G/RO/W/161). This modality compared the value of imports, which benefited from preferences, with the value of total imports, which would have been eligible for preferences. Hence, only tariff lines where there was a tariff preference were considered (that is, tariff lines that were either excluded from the preferential scheme or for which the MFN rate was zero were excluded from the calculations)."

In-person interviews with firms revealed that CO administration at the firm level is often handled by clerical staff and is driven primarily by buyer demands. In other words, compliance with rules of origin and the potential for duty savings do not seem to be part of senior management's focus or company policy in many of the Vietnamese firms interviewed. This in turn explains the mechanical approach to rules of origin management, where firms do not advocate for efficient reform of rules of origin and OPCs in public–private dialogue with the certifying authority.

Table 12: Viet Nam's Utilization Rate and Import Distribution by Tariff Treatment in the European Union Market, 2020–2022

	Imports ($ '000)							Utilization Rate	
Year	Total	Dutiable	GSP-Received	Other Preferences	All preferences (GSP + Other)	MFN/ RTAs	MFN Duty-Free	EU GSP (%)	EU-VIET FTA (%)
2022	52,658,684	22,923,906	5,438,456	9,574,484	15,012,940	7,910,966	29,734,778	24.49	42.49
2021	44,689,067	17,638,564	5,137,400	5, 571,375	10,708,774	6,929,789	27,050,504	30.91	33.30
2020	39,654,916	15,993,356	8,427,606	1,079,354	9,506,960	6,486,397	23,661,559	55.12	16.85

EU-GSP = European Union Generalized Scheme of Preferences, EU-VIET FTA = EU-Vietnam Free Trade Agreement, GSP = Generalized Scheme of Preferences, MFN = most favored nation, RTA = regional trade agreement.
Source: Authors based on Eurostat data.

Overall, the survey and its contextualization show that Vietnamese firms are face several challenges in complying with rules of origin, as reflected in the utilization rates. This finding calls for a review of the OCPs management in Viet Nam, with a view to foster the utilization of FTAs and maximize their benefits.

Finally, the questionnaire's findings support the benchmarks used in the coding exercise explained in Section 9.

9. Coding Operational Certification Procedures

The case for coding the various methods of proof of origin and OCPs is compelling, given the growing proliferation of overlapping initiatives, each claiming to be the most trade facilitating. The absence and protracted inability of the international community to even discuss, let alone agree on, best practices and lessons learned on proof of origin have created a no-man's-land, where the contest without an arbiter is generating confusion. In this contest, it is the ill-equipped countries that stand to lose.

This lack of common standards in a key area of regional trade integration in Asia and the Pacific is a gap that needs to be addressed. Progressive convergence toward a standard is a legitimate objective that should be pursued.

To this end, this study aims at providing a first elaboration of coding the different methods of proof of origin and OCP. This measures the existing provisions and practices adopted under ATIGA, ASEAN+1, RCEP, and CPTPP, by contrasting them with WCO guidelines and other multilateral benchmarks at WTO and UNCTAD, and the experience of practitioners and firms.

9.1 The Rationale for Coding

The motivation for coding is based on the need to establish a benchmark for measuring the trade-facilitating degree of various methods, practices, and provisions of proof of origin and OCP from the perspectives of WCO guidelines, practitioners, and firms' experiences. The coding will enable an initial assessment of different methods used as proof of origin and related OCPs to determine which FTA contains the most trade-facilitating provisions, what those provisions are, and what lessons can be learned from them. The objective is to provide policy and operational guidance to facilitate implementation of RCEP and other ASEAN+1 FTAs and a progressive convergence toward common standards.

9.2 The Coding Methodology

The main challenge of coding methods of proof of origin and OCPs is to measure a relatively limited number of observations responsible for a set of practices and requirements that are more or less trade facilitating. In addition, the observations are not product specific, in most cases, as they affect the cost of transactions across the board.

In the case of previous studies on product-specific rules of origin (PSROs), the number of observations were far greater, and the benchmark for measuring the restrictive or lenient nature of a PSRO was the level of manufacturing requirement necessary to comply with it (Crivelli, Inama, and Pearson 2022). This could be achieved with reasonable accuracy, as the measurement tools were linked to international benchmarks such as the Harmonized System[55] and arithmetical figures of regional value content or specific working and processing.

In the case of proof of origin and OCPs, the benchmarks are mostly provided by:

(a) intergovernmental practices and conventions mainly in WCO, WTO, and UNCTAD, or regional bodies as ASEAN (as discussed in Section 2);

(b) surveys, questionnaires, or other forms of testimony from firms;

(c) developments in customs administration as learning by doing; and

(d) utilization rates of trade preferences.

This list has to be read and understood with a series of qualifications.

Intergovernmental deliberations and consensus on methods of proof of origin at the WCO, WTO, and UNCTAD result from debates and negotiations arising from experience of administrations and governments gained over the years. Hence, the consensus from multilateral deliberations, as limited as they may be, should be treated with respect. For instance, paragraph 1.8 of the WTO Bali Decision on preferential rules of origin for least developed countries,[56] and paragraph 3 of the subsequent Nairobi decision[57] on the same subject, clearly identify self-certification, together with WCO guidelines on certification discussed in Section 4, as recommended practice.

The quality of firm's surveys and questionnaires heavily depends on the content of the questionnaire and how it has been administered when assembling the firms' responses. The results may be heavily influenced by regional aspects and the tendency to oversimplify the issues at stake to elicit responses. Section 8's extensive survey of more than 200 firms in Viet Nam was managed by a combination of online questionnaires and person-to-person interviews.

The individual or group testimony of firms that is cross-referenced with questionnaire results may provide valuable insights, especially when it is detailed and shows a precise case that a firm has faced—and, even more so, when it is not an isolated case. The benchmarks used for coding in this study have been peer reviewed by firms that have extensive knowledge of rules of origin and OCPs[58] and are part of the WCO's Regional Private Sector Group—Asia Pacific.[59]

Developments and improvements in the practices and laws of customs administration are also a valuable sign that certain practices are becoming obsolete and have caused difficulty. An example is the general movement away from the classical method of proof of origin on paper stamped with certifying

55 WCO. What is the Harmonized System (HS)? https://www.wcoomd.org/en/topics/nomenclature/overview/what-is-the-harmonized-system.aspx.

56 Paragraph 1.8 of Bali Decision provides as follows: *"The documentary requirements regarding compliance with the rules of origin should be simple and transparent. For instance, requirement to provide proof of non-manipulation or any other prescribed form for a certification of origin for products shipped from LDCs across other Members may be avoided. With regard to certification of rules of origin, whenever possible, self-certification may be recognized."*

57 "3. Documentary requirements 3.1. With a view to reducing the administrative burden related to documentary and procedural requirements related to origin, Preference-granting Members shall:
a) As a general principle, refrain from requiring a certificate of non-manipulation for products originating in a LDC but shipped across other countries unless there are concerns regarding transshipment, manipulation, or fraudulent documentation.
b) Consider other measures to further streamline customs procedures, such as minimizing documentation requirements for small consignments or allowing for self-certification."

58 For a series of testimonials of firms on rules of origin and OCPs, see Inama (2023).

59 WCO. 2021. Regional Private Sector Group Asia Pacific (RPSG-AP) Meeting. 29 July. https://www.wcoasiapacific.org/news/418-regional-private-sector-group-asia-pacific-rpsg-ap-meeting.

authority seals and certifying authority signatures, even if some administrations still use this method. The EU green paper of 2005 outlining reform of the administration of rules of origin was a tangible sign of how a government has been addressing possible options to reform its method of administering proof of origin and introduce REX as a new system.[60] The North American Trade Agreement also moved quickly away from certificates of origin to self-certification.

The Korea FTAPASS[61] is another example on how an administration has taken steps to facilitate firm's compliance with the growing complexity of rules of origin.

The utilization of trade preferences is a valuable benchmark based on customs data originally used by UNCTAD to monitor the effectiveness of trade preferences granted under the Generalized System of Preferences (GSP) (Inama 2022). Utilization rates have been used most recently in the context of the WTO Committee on Rules of Origin to monitor the utilization of trade preferences granted to LDCs. A series of submission by the LDC[62] have pointed out how the stringency or leniency of PSRO may determine utilization rates and trade flows as well as single OCPs provisions such as documentary evidence of direct consignment.[63] Also, a note by the WTO secretariat shows that preferential schemes granted to LDCs allowing for self-certification tend to be associated with higher levels of utilization than preferences requiring certificates of origin issued by certifying authorities.[64]

In the ASEAN context, Inama, Crivelli, and Ha (2022) pointed out that trade data from members reported in an ASEAN Secretariat study of 2021 show an average utilization rate of ATIGA trade preferences of 50% between 2019 and 2021. This appears to show that even the introduction of ATIGA Single Window in 2019 has not significantly improved utilization rates.

Even more astonishing, as discussed in Section 6, were ASEAN member states comments to this finding justifying that ATIGA utilization is low because many firms are using other ASEAN+1 FTAs for intra-ATIGA trade.

Bearing in mind this background and benchmarks, a qualitative analysis of the legal texts regulating the method of proof of origin and OCP provisions has been carried out to identify the trade-facilitating nature of the provisions and translate it into a numerical variable.

A comparative excel table has been built comparing the legal texts,including the various subcategories of the main OCP articles of selected FTAs.

Each of the proof of origin methods and related built-in provisions has been given a ranking from the most trade facilitating to the least trade facilitating according to qualitative criteria set in the coding rationale developed in this study for each of the categories and subcategories of OCP. The coding is structured in 16 categories and 19 subcategories, as detailed in Annex 1. Three examples of the coding procedure are provided below:

60 European Commission. 2005. *Communication from the Commission to the Council, The European Parliament and the European Economic and Social Committee, The rules of origin in preferential trade arrangements: Orientations for the future.* COM(2005) 100 final. Brussels, March 16, 2005.

61 See: https://ftapass.or.kr/site/english/page/register/viewBasic.do.

62 See Compendium of technical notes prepared for the LDC WTO Group on preferential rules of origin (I) https://unctad.org/system/files/official-document/aldc2020d6_en.pdf and (II) https://unctad.org/system/files/official-document/aldc2022d6_en.pdf.

63 See WTO Document G/RO/W/186.

64 See WTO Document (G/RO/W/212).

- Self-certification by exporter is more trade facilitating than CO issued and stamped by a certifying authority.
- Registered exporter is more trade facilitating than approved exporter.
- A CO form with more than 13 entries is less trade facilitating than one with less than 13 entries.

The ranking has been assigned in descending order, where 0 or 1 is the most trade-facilitating method or single provision, and scores get progressively higher if the method or provision is less trade facilitating compared with other methods. Where there is no provision or method, this is indicated with "not applicable."

The ranking of the most or less trade-facilitating provisions has been assigned on the basis of the consideration and qualitative criteria discussed in Sections 2 to 6. The score is calculated as 1 or 0 being the most trade facilitating and a higher number (2, 3, or more) progressively less trade facilitating. For provisions coded as being equivalent across FTAs, the same score has been assigned.

In some cases, it has been necessary to split into subcategories the various elements that constitute a single provision or method of proof of origin. A case in point is the method where, besides providing a general score for the most trade-facilitating method, it has been necessary to break the proof of origin method into subcategories to capture the different requirements that may apply within a single category. This has been especially the case for FTAs that still provide for a specific CO form in which the specific entries are heavily regulated.

A complicating factor of the ranking, in addition to the difficulty of identifying the latest legal text in force,[65] derives from the different method of proof of origin provided in legal text with different phase-in periods. The CPTPP and RCEP are the most striking examples.

The CPTPP main legal text provides in article 3.24 for an importer-based method of proof of origin. Yet, Annex 3A, which will be in force for 12 years, is authorizing CPTPP parties to apply alternative methods such a CO issued by a competent authority or a CO issued by approved exporters. Similarly, RCEP adopts in article 3.17 a method based on (i) COs issued by a certifying authority, (ii) a declaration of origin by an approved exporter, and (iii) a declaration of origin by any exporter. Yet, further provisions in RCEP legal text provide that the implementation of (c) may take up to 30 years for LDC RCEP parties. The implementation of approved exporters in RCEP is subject according to paragraph 6 of article 3.18 to the establishment of the approved exporter database, which shall be accessible online by the RCEP parties. A three-page long document on the provisional RCEP secretariat website on the RCEP Parties' and Signatory States' Status on CO Issuance and CO/DO Acceptance at the EIF (as of 8 February 2022) does not mention or refer to the website of registered exporters.[66] This is consistent with the hesitation among ASEAN member states to adopt the approved exporter method.

In the context of these uncertainties, it is understandable the hesitation demonstrated during the testimony of two firms in using RCEP and CPTPP and the low utilization rates that these two mega-regional agreements are recording so far (Anliker 2023, Hickey 2023).[67]

[65] The public availability and accessibility of ATIGA and ASEAN+ 1 FTA legal text has been a persistent issue for decades: See Inama and Sim (2015).

[66] RCEP Parties' and Signatory States' Status on CO Issuance and CO/DO Acceptance at the EIF (as of 15 July 2024) at https://rcepsec.org/wp-content/uploads/2024/08/6-RCEP-Parties-and-Signatory-States-Status-on-electronic-CO-issuance-and-PO-acceptance_15-August-2024-rev.pdf.

[67] Utilization rates will be further discussed in a forthcoming ADB publication on Cambodia graduation from least developed countries.

To accurately rank this complex landscape, factoring in implementation status, each method's ranking has been adjusted accordingly. For example, while the CPTPP would initially rank as 1 due to its legal text specifying an importer-based method, Annex 3A of the CPTPP also allows a certification issued by a certifying authority and an approved exporter. This means that +6 points and +3 points should be added to 1, making a total of 10 points, since the importer-based methodology will not be widely adopted by many partners for the next 12 years. It is important to highlight that such inconsistencies among legal text and practice or different implementation timelines are not limited to this example alone.

For instance, the EU–Viet Nam provides for the REX system for both parties. However, Viet Nam is yet to notify the EU that it intends to implement the REX system, while the EU already did the other way around. This means that the REX system is applicable in the direction of trade from EU to Viet Nam, but for the direction of trade from Viet Nam to the EU the hard copy of FORM EUR 1 still applicable.

As discussed in Section 6, whereas the implementation of Form D in the ASEAN Single Window was declared fully implemented at the beginning of 2024, field visits have ascertained that the reality may be different. In addition, various forms of bilateral e-COs are accepted within ASEAN+1 FTAs since a series of bilateral memorandums of understanding have been entered to this effect. To the extent possible, and considering the availability of information, these various factors have been accounted for in assigning different rankings.

9.3 Results of the Coding

9.3.1 Cumulative proof of origin methods

Table 13 shows the results of a cumulative ranking by each certification used, considering the differences in phasing in different methods of proof of origin and implementation issues. ATIGA ranks as most complicated, with 14 points accumulated due to overlapping. An empty box means that the FTA does not use the corresponding method of proof of origin.

The EU–Viet Nam FTA ranks second in complexity due to the overlapping method of proof of origin, which vary depending on the direction of trade. AANZFTA ranks third, given the lengthy implementation period of its more trade-facilitating methods of approved exporter or any exporter (up to 30 years). AKFTA also ranks third, since the signing of bilateral memorandum of understanding allowing the use of e-COs intended as a scan or PDF version of Form AK, may lead to overlap and create uncertainty. ACFTA and AJCEP rank fourth, as their method of proof origin still rely on hard-copy COs. Finally, the EU-Singapore FTA, having fully implemented the REX system, one of the more trade-facilitating methods, ranks as the easiest to comply with, alongside the EU-Japan FTA, using a combination of importer-based certification and registered exporters.[68] Under AKFTA, the Republic of Korea and Viet Nam, and the Republic of Korea and Indonesia are accepting scanned copy or PDF of Form AK. To the extent possible the ranking of Table 13 has taken into account of such differences.

[68] The EU-Japan FTA provides for a combined proof of origin based on a registered exporter declaration and an importer-knowledge based declaration. While such alternative methods of self-certification may appear liberal and have been cited as one of the models to adopt, experience suggests that adequate provisions must be inserted in the OCPs' legal texts to clarify certain aspects of these dual OCPs methods. In fact both the EU and Japan had to publish additional guidelines to better explain and clarify the concrete functioning of such dual system. See for the EU: https://taxation-customs.ec.europa.eu/system/files/2019-12/eu-japan-epa-guidance-statements-on-origin.pdf see for Japan https://www.customs.go.jp/roo/procedure/riyou_eu_EN.pdf.

Table 13: Overall Ranking Based on Cumulative Calculation of Methods of Proof of Origin

Main methodologies of proof of origin	Ranking assigned	ATIGA	AANZFTA	ACFTA	AJCEP	AKFTA	EUSIN	EUVIE	EUJAP	CPTPP	RCEP
Methods based on self-certification											
Certificate of origin signed by any exporter	1		X								
Importer declaration	1								X	X	X
Statement of origin by registered exporters	2						X	X	X		
Statement of origin by approved exporters	3	X	X					X		X	X
Methods based on the existence of a Certifying authority.											
e-COs	4					X					
e-COs via ASEAN single windows	5	X									
Certificate of origin stamped and signed by certifying authorities	6	X	X	X	X	X		X		X	X
Total		**14**	**10**	**6**	**6**	**10**	**2**	**11**	**3**	**10**	**10**

AANZFTA = ASEAN-Australia-New Zealand Free Trade Area, ACFTA = ASEAN–China Free Trade Area, AJCEP = ASEAN–Japan Comprehensive Economic Partnership, AKFTA = ASEAN–Korea Free Trade, ASEAN = Association of Southeast Asian Nations, ATIGA = ASEAN Trade in Goods Agreement, CPTPP = Comprehensive and Progressive Agreement for Trans-Pacific Partnership, e-CO = electronic certificate of origin, EUJAP = EU-Japan Economic Partnership Agreement, EUSIN = EU-Singapore Free Trade Agreement, EUVIE = EU-Vietnam Free Trade Agreement, RCEP = Regional Comprehensive Economic Partnership.
Source: Authors.

This ranking should be interpreted with caution, acknowledging its limitations. For example, some FTAs, such AANZA, have demonstrated a clear commitment to move toward more trade-facilitating procedures and self-certification.

9.3.2 Coding proof of origin methods and individual provisions

Table 14 presents the overall results, summing up the points assigned by coding the proof of origin methods (Table 15) along with those assigned to the coding of the single provisions (Table 16). ATIGA and RCEP are ranked as the most complex FTAs, with scores of 45 and 44 points, respectively. The use of CO Forms with complicated entry requirements significantly contributes to these high rankings. Except for AANZFTA, all other ASEAN+1 FTAs score above 30 points, with ACFTA and AJCEP both

Table 14: Ranking Grand Total Calculating Method of Proof of Origin and Single Provisions

	ATIGA	AANZFTA	ACFTA	AJCEP	AKFTA	EUSIN	EUVIE	EUJAP	CPTPP	RCEP
Grand Total	45	28	37	37	32	11	21	13	24	44

AANZFTA = ASEAN-Australia-New Zealand Free Trade Area, ACFTA = ASEAN–China Free Trade Area, AJCEP = ASEAN–Japan Comprehensive Economic Partnership, AKFTA = ASEAN–Korea Free Trade, ATIGA = ASEAN Trade in Goods Agreement, CPTPP = Comprehensive and Progressive Agreement for Trans-Pacific Partnership, EUJAP = EU-Japan Economic Partnership Agreement, EUSIN = EU-Singapore Free Trade Agreement, EUVIE = EU-Vietnam Free Trade Agreement, RCEP = Regional Comprehensive Economic Partnership.
Source: Authors.

scoring 37 points, ranking just below ATIGA and RCEP. In contrast, the EU FTAs with Japan, Singapore, and Viet Nam are among the most trade-facilitative agreements, with the EU-Singapore FTA leading with only 11 points. The CPTPP also ranks relatively low in complexity, scoring 24 points.

Table 15 shows the results based on the complexity of implementing each method of proof origin available in different FTAs. ATIGA's implementation of COs scores the highest with 19 points, surpassing all other ASEAN+1 FTAs. AJCEP ranks second, while RCEP and ACFTA share third place with 15 points.

Table 15: FTAs Ranking by the Complexity of Each Method of Proof of Origin Used

	ATIGA	AANZFTA	ACFTA	AJCEP	AKFTA	EUSIN	EUVIE	EUJAP	CPTPP	RCEP
Certificate of Origin	19	10	15	18	14	NA	6	NA	4	15
Registered exporters	NA	NA	NA	NA	NA	1	2	1	NA	NA
Approved exporter	4	3	NA	NA	NA	NA*	2	NA	4	4
Any exporter	NA	NA	NA	NA	NA	NA	NA	NA	2	4
Importer declaration	NA	NA	NA	NA	NA	NA	NA	2	3	3
CO by single window	1	NA	NA	NA	NA	NA	NA	NA	NA	NA
Total	**24**	**13**	**15**	**18**	**14**	**1**	**10**	**3**	**13**	**26**

AANZFTA = ASEAN-Australia-New Zealand Free Trade Area, ACFTA = ASEAN–China Free Trade Area, AJCEP = ASEAN–Japan Comprehensive Economic Partnership, AKFTA = ASEAN–Korea Free Trade, ATIGA = ASEAN Trade in Goods Agreement, CO = certificate of origin, CPTPP = Comprehensive and Progressive Agreement for Trans-Pacific Partnership, EUJAP = EU-Japan Economic Partnership Agreement, EUSIN = EU-Singapore Free Trade Agreement, EUVIE = EU-Vietnam Free Trade Agreement, FTA = free trade agreement, NA = not applicable, RCEP = Regional Comprehensive Economic Partnership.
* From 1 January 2023 the approved exporter method has been replaced by REX see https://taxation-customs.ec.europa.eu/news/eu-preferential-exports-singapore-shall-be-covered-statements-origin-made-out-registered-exporters-1-2022-12-21_en
Source: Authors.

ATIGA also ranks as the most complicated FTA when using an approved exporter method under the ASEAN-wide Self-Certification scheme.[69] Implementation of any exporter self-certification is included in RCEP; however the long transition period of 10 years for some RCEP parties, and 20 years for others, with the option to extend by a potential additional 10 years results in a score of 4. In comparison, the faster implementation of 12 years under the CPTPP scores 2. RCEP ranks as the most complicated FTA overall for proof of origin methods, with the highest total score, followed by ATIGA.

[69] See *ASEAN-wide Self-Certification Guidebook* available at https://asean.org/wp-content/uploads/2021/09/ASEAN-wide-Self-Certification-Guidebook-web.pdf.

Table 16 shows results by ranking each main provision, with ACFTA emerging as the most complicated FTA in terms of OCP with 22 points, followed by ATIGA with 21. RCEP with 18 points does not show a significant improvement, while CPTPP and the EU FTAs show much better scores.

Despite the challenges and complexities of the coding exercise, the ranking results are in line with the qualitative analysis and comparison of the different legal texts undertaken in this study. In addition, the results of the coding match those undertaken under previous studies on PSRO.

ATIGA ranks as having the most complex method of administering rules of origin and single OCP provisions, followed by RCEP. The results of the coding and the qualitative analysis clearly indicates that the reason underpinning this score is due to the overlapping of existing methods of proof of origin, a two-tier implementation reality where the ASEAN LDCs are not up to speed with more-developed member states, and a set of single OCP provisions that are not in line with more modern or trade-facilitating practices such as those contained in CPTPP. RCEP, an FTA that was expected to cut short the red tape caused by overlapping FTAs, ranks the second most complicated, as it largely inherited the deficiencies and piecemeal approach adopted in ATIGA. The other ASEAN+1 FTAs are showing isolated, tentative indications of trade facilitation by accepting an e-CO that is a PDF version of the scanned hard-copy CO form. This, however, represents a form of trade facilitation that is too little and too late.

Table 16: FTAs Ranking by Single Provision

		ATIGA	AANZFTA	ACFTA	AJCEP	AKFTA	EUSIN	EUVIE	EUJAP	CPTPP	RCEP
Back-to-back		2	1	3	2	2	0	0	0	0	2
Third-party invoice		2	1	2	2	2	0	0	1	1	2
Direct consignment		2	2	3	3	2	0	0	0	1	1
Small consignments		2	1	2	1	1	0	0	0	0	1
Cumulation	Main	3	2	4	3	3	2	3	2	2	4
	Suppliers Documents	1	0	0	0	0	1	1	1	0	0
	Implementation Issues	2	3	2	2	2	1	2	0	1	4
	Subtotal	6	5	6	5	5	4	6	3	3	8
Drawback		1	2	2	2	2	3	2	2	2	2
Advance Rulings		2	0	1	1	1	2	2	2	2	1
Accounting Segregation		0	0	0	0	0	1	1	1	0	0
Record-keeping		1	1	1	1	1	0	0	0	1	0
Verification		3	2	2	2	2	0	0	1	1	1
Total		21	15	22	19	18	10	11	10	11	18

AANZFTA = ASEAN-Australia-New Zealand Free Trade Area, ACFTA = ASEAN–China Free Trade Area, AJCEP = ASEAN–Japan Comprehensive Economic Partnership, AKFTA = ASEAN–Korea Free Trade, ATIGA = ASEAN Trade in Goods Agreement, CPTPP = Comprehensive and Progressive Agreement for Trans-Pacific Partnership, EUJAP = EU-Japan Economic Partnership Agreement, EUSIN = EU-Singapore Free Trade Agreement, EUVIE = EU-Vietnam Free Trade Agreement, FTA = free trade agreement, RCEP = Regional Comprehensive Economic Partnership.
Source: Authors.

10. Findings and Recommendations

Overall, the analysis in this study detected a persistent preference in ASEAN toward the involvement of certifying authorities or government agencies in the management of proof of origin. This preference has had influence on countries throughout Asia and the Pacific when negotiating FTAs with ASEAN as a group. The comparative analysis of legal texts and codification of FTA provisions match the firms' survey results and the views of trade practitioners in the region, showing that ASEAN as a group is wedded to the provisions or legislation designed in the ATIGA, negotiated in 2009. As a customary practice, ASEAN has been using the ATIGA template to negotiate ASEAN-plus FTAs, with ATIGA in its original 2009 version centered on the use of certifying authority for issuing certificates of origin (COs) (Inama and Sim 2015).

ASEAN member states and the ASEAN Secretariat coordinated their positions in ASEAN+1 FTA negotiations based on a model of proof or origin that relies on the use of a certifying authority, as outlined in ATIGA. However, when ASEAN member states negotiated FTAs independently of ASEAN, they accepted the self-declaration approach or options that included self-certification. This approach featured in the Malaysia-New Zealand FTA, the New Zealand-Thailand FTA, the CPTPP, and New Zealand-Singapore Closer Economic Partnership (CEP).

- Malaysia–New Zealand FTA: Declaration of origin by the exporter or producer, or a CO for exports from Malaysia.
- New Zealand–Thailand CEP: Self-declaration by the exporter, producer, or a competent person.
- CPTPP: Self declaration by the exporter or producer, or a certificate of origin.
- New Zealand–Singapore CEP: Self-certification by the exporter, producer, or importer.

Four ASEAN member states, as CPTPP partners, have accepted more liberal provisions on self-certification compared to those typically contained in the ASEAN+1 FTAs, although with extended transition periods.

ASEAN has made efforts to move away from a certification system based on CO and certifying authorities, and shift toward self-certification (Inama and Sim 2015). However, this transition has been lengthy and complex as evidenced by the ASEAN guidebook, which reported 550 certified exporters across the region as of September 2020.[70] Furthermore, the recent member states' focus on utilizing ATIGA Form D through the ASEAN Single Window is a positive step. However, as discussed in this study, it also presents challenges and has not led to an increase in ATIGA utilization rates. The signing of bilateral memorandums of understanding for the application of OCPs through national single windows, without coordinated regional efforts, risks creating a new layer of complexity through the proliferation of bilateral proof of origin systems. This study's findings suggest that uncoordinated digitalization of

[70] See *ASEAN-wide Self-Certification (AWSC) Guidebook*, 2020.

proof of origin and OCP is contributing to an additional noodle bowl of OCPs, adding to the challenges posed by the existing tangle of PSROs.

It is recommended that countries in Asia and the Pacific converge on a series of best practices, especially on proof of origin and OCPs as well as on digitalization initiatives. Both the RCEP and CPTPP mega-regional agreements contain provisions—as examined in this study—for self-certification that major trading partners, with the exception of the PRC, also use.[71]

ASEAN member states and other countries in Asia and the Pacific should consider lessons learned and best practices from other administrations and international organizations. The complexity in implementing ATIGA and ASEAN+1 FTAs is widely documented, and has been raised not only in the Sub-committee on ATIGA Rules of Origin but also by the private sector (see Box 5 for a firm's perspective on simplifying OCPs). Alternatives that address such persistent implementation difficulties should be found within the ASEAN intergovernmental machinery.

It is recommended that ASEAN and its Asia and Pacific partners engage in developing uniform regulations for the interpretation, application, and administration of the protocols on rules of origin and OCP in ATIGA and ASEAN+1 FTAs, following the model of the North American Free Trade Agreement or NAFTA and its successor, the US–Mexico–Canada Agreement.[72] Such engagement would establish uniform standards for the implementation of the different protocols of rules of origin and OCPs, aiming at eliminating divergences among existing practices deployed by national customs authorities.

Moreover, as provided for in many of the FTAs examined in this study, self-certification should be the convergence area. Such an option would also allow increased investment of resources in human capacity (capacity building of customs officials and firms). The experience of the Republic of Korea and Japan customs in this area could be explored in ways and means that help firms and customs implement self-certification. Self-certification should be accompanied by capacity building and training for rules of origin and OCP programs.

Such programs can help create an informed and efficient trade environment, reducing errors and compliance costs while promoting effective trade flows. By equipping stakeholders with necessary skills and knowledge, these initiatives ensure the successful implementation of trade agreements.

A structured training plan targeted to customs authorities and businesses involved in international trade is needed to achieve this. The plan could include regular workshops, seminars, and training sessions on rules of origin and OCPs, covering the latest developments in electronic certification systems like the ASEAN Single Window and self-certification methods. Also, online training modules and resources and up-to-date and fully functional government websites can provide continuous learning opportunities. Collaboration with international trade organizations and experienced trainers can improve the quality and relevance of programs and ensure stakeholders are well prepared to navigate modern trade regulations and procedures.

Self-certification would move the focus away from CO documentation and toward the fundamentals of the transaction. Traders/exporters/importers could provide a statement/declaration about the origin of the product in question on the invoice, and customs could use risk assessment techniques and post-

[71] As discussed in Box 4, the PRC has elaborated a version of self-certification that differs substantially from the common notion of self-certification.

[72] See https://ustr.gov/sites/default/files/files/agreements/FTA/USMCA/Text/UniformRegulations.pdf.

clearance recovery where incorrect or fraudulent origin declarations were made. While maintaining a substantial degree of reliability, such system would be simpler and more cost-effective, and therefore support Asia and Pacific economies in reaping higher benefits form FTAs in the region.

Box 5: A Way Forward Toward Simplifying OCPs—Perspectives from the Private Sector

Trade facilitation should be the **key guiding principle** to be followed. However, it seems that many associations or government institutions are more focused on setting up individual complex creative rules responding to vested interests and ignoring efforts of other countries or institutions on the same topic. As a result, there is a conspicuous overlapping and little cooperation. The rules of thumb should be that it really does not make sense to negotiate a free trade agreement (FTA) and then make it administratively so complicated that it becomes almost a trade barrier.

Suggested way forward:

Post-import audits and verifications should be the focus. Let the imports take place at preferential rate, and then audit firms using risks assessment methods, investigating at that moment if the formal certificates of origin (COs) are right in place, and if the origin calculations are made in a correct manner, supported by the right documentation. This post-import approach coupled with a simplified self-declaration process would be highly trade facilitating.

Utilization rates and complexity of rules of origin and OCPs

The overcomplicating noodle bowls of different rules and processes do automatically lead to underutilization of FTAs by companies. Why? Because in today's business world, using FTAs has to respond to efficiency criteria: in most instances, a monetary business case must be presented within the firm to convince the upper management to invest into a proper Origin Management.

Origin has to be automated because of the high volume of transactions; for large firms, anything manual is difficult to manage. The IT systems already existing in firms are often highly complex and much less developed than it may be imagined making management of new topics, such rules of origin and OCPs very challenging.

If we want to make FTAs work and automation applied, companies need standard drafting models from FTAs, e.g., those drafting models/rules can be easily translated from the legal into the IT world. By increasing the complexities of OCPs, and many other FTA-specific provisions such as product-specific rules of origin (PSRO), a firm would have to spend for every single FTA more money to adjust the IT system than the duties that can be saved. This results in companies not using FTAs. It is as simple as that.

Suggested way forward: this challenge can be addressed with a convergence of PSRO and OCP negotiated with a highly ambitious and trade facilitation mindset.

Lack of training, education, and alignment between businesses and governments

One of the key issues that leads to the misalignments and current noodle bowl of misunderstandings is the lack of training and education coupled with the low level of knowledge of many stakeholders from business as well as government side. The misuse and misunderstandings of legal terms and procedures contained in FTAs leads to misinterpretation of many business practices.

This is due to the fact that the large majority of stakeholders participating in rules of origin negotiations, workshops, or discussions aiming at setting best practices possess little knowledge about business processes and/or little "technical" expertise on the know-how of the practical application of what they are discussing.

continued on the next page

Box 5 continued.

A testing ground would be to organize a one-to-one specific exchange among officials negotiating FTAs, and discussing and establishing OCPs, with a group of firms on how certain practices or rules may be applied in practice. Perhaps such dialogue may lead to less divergence. It has to be realized that a mindset such as "if companies want to use our FTA, they just have to adapt" will not work, since there are too many FTAs and companies will just use the most advantageous, if any.

Suggested way forward: a consistent and holistic in depth origin research and capacity-building program is required to be funded from aid for trade funds available for firms as well as government officials, to **understand the details of FTAs as well as business operations**, and the implications what kind of rules may have on firms operations.

Impractical rules of origin impeding utilization of FTAs for firms

As highlighted in Crivelli and Inama (2022), megaregionals such as the Regional Comprehensive Economic Partnership (RCEP), which were expected to address the existing 'noodle bowl' of rules of origin, often demonstrate complexities, as seen in the case of RCEP where almost every partner maintains its own headnotes, tariff commitments, and tariff differentials. This is an example of a very cumbersome way implementing an FTA. It is extremely challenging to implement such rules from a firm perspective: a firm has to investigate applicable provisions for every RCEP country to identify what rule is applicable. So the question returns: why undertake efforts to put together such a great agreement with so many partners, but then make it so unpractical to use with unnecessary trade barriers?

In addition, it is confusing that certain FTAs have separate annexes for OCPs, while in other FTAs OCPs are part of the FTA text (like RCEP). Operational topics should be all in the same document as it would help businesses to understand what is expected.

Conclusion:

- The complexity of OCPs in FTAs is increasing, and the trend goes into more complexity – this has to addressed if firms are expected to utilize FTAs.
- A plurilateral or multilateral initiative is needed, inspired to a new mindset, a clean slate to identify a **global toolbox where** authorities may adopt **one single trade-facilitating system** based on **self-declaration** for proofs of origin, coupled with **proper enforcement and post-import audit culture**.
- **Such approach may not lead to harmonization but rather to convergence, inspired to the principle that is more efficient and cost-saving to establish a framework of legal requirements for a self-certification process, rather** having authorities putting so many efforts into the formal rules of how a document must look like.
- Such efforts should lead to setting up **clear standardized best practices that are recommended to be negotiated in the FTAs (e.g., best practices of back-to-back, third-party invoicing, etc.)**, clearly pointing out unnecessary provisions that are impractical, not connected to the operational logistics reality, not formally excessive.

CO = certificate of origin, FTA = free trade agreement, OCP = operational certification procedure, PSRO = product-specific rules of origin, RCEP = Regional Comprehensive Economic Partnership, RoO = rules of origin.
Source: Authors using contributions from firms.

References

Anliker, M. 2023. How Firms Assess the Case for Using New FTAs: The Regional Comprehensive Economic Partnership (RCEP). In S. Inama, ed. *Rules of Origin: Firm Perspectives, Lessons Learned, and Ways Forward.* European University Institute.

ASEAN Secretariat. 2020. *ASEAN-Wide Self-Certification (AWSC) Guidebook.*

Crivelli, P., and S. Inama. 2022. A Preliminary Assessment of the Regional Comprehensive Economic Partnership. *ADB Briefs.* No. 206. January.

Crivelli, P. and S. Inama. 2022. Disciplining rules of origin at the multilateral level towards open and inclusive global value chains. *T20 Indonesia Task Force 1 Policy Brief.* Policy Brief. September. https://www.global-solutions-initiative.org/wp-content/uploads/2022/11/TF1_Disciplining_rules_of_origin_at_the_multilateral_level_towards_open_and_inclusive_global_value_chains.pdf.

Crivelli, P., S. Inama, and M. Pearson. 2022. *An Analysis of the Product-Specific Rules of Origin of the Regional Comprehensive Economic Partnership.* Asian Development Bank. http://dx.doi.org/10.22617/TCS220167-2.

Crivelli, P., S. Inama, and M. Pearson. 2023. *An Assessment of Rules of Origin in RCEP and ASEAN+ 1 Free Trade Agreements.* Asian Development Bank.

Deloitte. 2021. *Customs authorities announce measures to implement RCEP rules of origin.* https://www.taxathand.com/article/20685/China-Peoples-Republic-of/2021/Customs-authorities-announce-measures-to-implement-RCEP-rules-of-origin.

European Commission. 2005. *Communication from the Commission to the Council, The European Parliament and the European Economic and Social Committee, The rules of origin in preferential trade arrangements: Orientations for the future.* COM(2005) 100 final. Brussels, March 16, 2005.

General Administration of Customs of the People's Republic of China. 2021. *Order No. 254: Measures of the Customs of the People's Republic of China for the Administration of Approved Exporters.* November 23. https://www-lawinfochina-com.translate.goog/display.aspx?id=37026&lib=law&_x_tr_sch=http&_x_tr_sl=zh-CN&_x_tr_tl=en&_x_tr_hl=en&_x_tr_pto=sc.

Hickey, K. 2023. RCEP and CPTPP: Building Blocks of Convergence? Or Another Brick in the Wall for Existing FTA Network. In S. Inama, ed. *Rules of Origin: Firm Perspectives, Lessons Learned, and Ways Forward.* European University Institute.

Inama, S. 2023. *Rules of Origin in International Trade* (2nd edition). Cambridge University Press.

Inama, S., ed. 2023. *Rules of Origin: Firm Perspectives, Lessons Learned, and Ways Forward.* European University Institute. https://cadmus.eui.eu/bitstream/handle/1814/76084/Rules_of_origin_Book_2023.pdf?sequence=2&isAllowed=y.

Inama, S. and E.W. Sim. 2015. *Rules of Origin in ASEAN: A Way Forward.* Cambridge University Press. https://doi.org/10.1017/CBO9781316145128.

Inama, S., P. Crivelli, and P. M. Ha. 2022. The Low Use by Firms of ASEAN Trade Preferences: Will RCEP Follow the Same Destiny? An Agenda for Rescue to Reform Rules of Origin in the Asian and Pacific Region. *Global Trade and Customs Journal.* 17(6): 248–51.

Trabucco, M. 2023. The Experience of Applying Rules of Origin: A View from the Private Sector. In S. Inama, ed. *Rules of Origin: Firm Perspectives, Lessons Learned, and Ways Forward.* European University Institute.

United States Agency for International Development (USAID). 2016. Self-Certification in ASEAN: An Assessment of Philippine Implementation of the Second ASEAN Self-Certification Process. 3 March.

World Customs Organization (WCO). 2018. Guidelines on Certification of Origin. https://www.wcoomd.org/-/media/wco/public/global/pdf/topics/key-issues/revenue-package/guidelines-on-certification.pdf.

________. 2024a. Draft Summary Findings of Study on the Digitalization of the Certificate of Origin. Annex to Doc. OC0253E.

________. 2024b. Feasibility Study on Interconnectivity Framework for Certificates of Origin based on the Globally Networked Customs (GNC) Methodologies. Annex to Doc. OC0254Ea.

Appendix: Detailed Breakdown of Origin Certification, Exporter Registration, and Related Procedures

Category	Subcategory
1. Certificate of Origin	
	1.1.1 Name of form
	1.1.2 Specimen
	1.1.3 Format
	1.1.4 Copies
	1.1.5 Distribution of copies
	1.1.6 Duplicates
	1.1.7 Retrospectives
	1.1.8 Number of Entries
1.2 Entry in box 8	
	(Box 10 in RCEP)
	1.2.1 Goods wholly obtained or produced
	1.2.2 Goods entirely produced
	1.2.3 Regional value content
	1.2.4 Change in tariff classification
	1.2.5 Specific processes
	1.2.6 Combination criteria
	1.2.7 Product specific requirement
1.3 BOX 13	
	1.3.1 Partial cumulation (PC)
	1.3.2 De minimis
	1.3.3 Accumulation
	1.3.3 Tariff differentials
TOTAL	
2. Registered exporters	
	2.1 Provisions
	2.1 Text of the Origin declaration
	2.2 Manuscript signature
TOTAL	

Category	Subcategory
3. Approved Exporter	
	3.1 Provision
	3.2 Text of the Declaration
	3.3 Manuscript Signature
TOTAL	
4. Any exporter	
	4.1 Provision
	4.2 Text of Declaration
	4.3 Manuscript Signature
TOTAL	
5. Importer declaration	
TOTAL	
6. Certificate of origin by single window	
TOTAL	
7. Back-to-back	
8. Third party	
9. Direct consignment	
	9.1 Main
	9.2 Evidence
10. Small consignments	
11. Cumulation	
	11.1 Main
	11.2 Supplies Documents
	11.3 Implementation Issues
Subtotal	
12. Drawback	
13. Advance Rulings	
14. Accounting Segregation	
15. Record-keeping	
16. Verification	

www.ingramcontent.com/pod-product-compliance
Lightning Source LLC
Chambersburg PA
CBHW041757220926
51847CB00014B/238